Horse Cents

A Sensible Guide for the Equestrian Enthusiast

Millie Chalk

Deborah Dawn, Editor

ISBN: 0615663893
ISBN-13: 978-0615663890

Disclaimer of Liability: Horse care and riding are not without risk, and while the author, editor and publisher have made every attempt to offer accurate and reliable information to the best of their knowledge and belief, it is presented without any guarantee. The author, editor and publisher therefore disclaim any liability incurred in connection with using the information contained in this book.

Cover photo: Baby Doll is an exquisite young thoroughbred whose fate smiled kindly upon her the day Sue and Kenny Chandler opened their hearts and their minds to the possibility of horse ownership. Baby Doll is a wonderful example of what miraculous possibilities love can bring.

DEDICATION

I'd like to dedicate this book to all of the four leggeds who I've known that have offered me unconditional love while teaching me life lessons in kindness, patience and understanding. To their people that realize that there's always something more to learn. I dedicate not only my book but my life in pursuing new and innovative ways to teach what empowers others to care and care for. I will strive to keep my mind open to what I can learn each new day and share what works to further the cause of excellent horse management.

To Misty, Oreo, Princess, Cookie Monster, Devlan, Tiffany, Sea Breeze, Rai, 2nd Tiffany, Clementine and Winston; the ponies and horses, most now past, that carried my precious daughter to victories both physically and emotionally, challenging her spirit and boosting her confidence while keeping her safe, I owe my extreme adoration and appreciation.

Lastly I'd like to thank everything that has come to my life both good and bad that has brought me to this place in my experience so that I might bring about this work and to all of those that have inspired me and supported me in the writing of this book.

CONTENTS

FOREWORD

Why horses? When you look at all the different things people can gravitate to there is hardly an interest as compelling as being with horses. Throughout history, people kept horses for practical reasons and although I can only assume there were times that an owner would become attached to their mount, it has only been recently that everyday people have afforded themselves the luxury of owning a horse for no reason other than the sheer enjoyment of riding and interacting with such a magnificent animal. Even if an owner saves some money by caring for their horse themselves, it's still a rather cost prohibitive sport. With monthly horse expenses costing some families above and beyond things such as their mortgage, it makes one wonder why we do it? What compels people to go without, sometimes even the necessities of life, just so they can keep their horses? And then there are the safety issues. What drives a person, often with no experience whatsoever, to want to have that personal interaction with such an enormous creature; one that although labeled domestic is still quite tapped into their primal instincts?

Being with horses isn't for everyone. I've always recognized there are those who want nothing to do with the animal outside of an occasional pet and the offering of an apple. So when most of the population doesn't really care if you have horse experience, what drives the reasonably few of us to give up so much of our time, our money and our security to be around these animals? There are probably as many answers to this question as there are horse enthusiasts. Some people thrill at the possibility of a connection to such a noble creature, others love the physical experience of feeling a thousand pounds of flesh moving freely underneath them with only the illusion of control offered through a rider's hands. There are those that can appreciate that riding a horse keeps you in the moment, rather like a moving meditation. In reference to that, Winston Churchill once wrote, "there is something about the outside of a horse that is good for the inside of a man." I feel the most common reason for us to love our horses is that for some of us it simply is in our blood.

Have you ever noticed how "horse fever" seems to be hereditary? How one child can be stricken within a family, but not their sibling only to find out there was a parent or an Aunt or an Uncle that was an avid horseperson, as well? Personally, I found a good many horse people in my family, even some generations ago that died in the State Penitentiary for being horse thieves. Now that's a serious obsession! I have to admit I have had horses in my past that I would gladly go to jail for. Our horses become members of our families just as much as the family dog or cat or maybe even more so.

I've owned horses all of my life and even though I'm as hooked as the next person, I'm still amazed at how much we're willing to sacrifice to get our horse fix. What I've found throughout all of my years working around horses is that our desired experiences for life can change but we always manage to weave our horses into the equation. So to all of those that I share this kinship with, always remember to lead from your heart, open your mind and let your intuition guide you to the information and to those that would keep what's best for you and your horse foremost in their minds.

Happy horse keeping!

INTRODUCTION

There are those out there that teach the concept that you create your experience with your thoughts. There are also those that teach that your horse experience is simply a reflection of your life in general. If these two concepts are true then indeed you should feel very gratified that your energy has attracted this book to you. My hope is that when you read my words, you will feel as though you are conversing with a friend, a good friend; that cares the utmost about you, and your horse, and wants to see you succeed in your pursuit of excellence in horse care.

Owning up to the responsibility of creating your life's experience is liberating, and often rewarding, and finding yourself now solely in charge, (or even partially), of your equestrian experience is just as gratifying. Becoming the one that knows your horse better than any other person is the ultimate in horse ownership satisfaction; and I would challenge anyone, (that has received proper guidance), to be happy going back to letting someone else make those daily, life altering decisions. Thinking of professionals having total control over their client's horse brings to mind images I've witnessed over the years, while at competitions or visiting other facilities, where an owner is clueless. They and their horse are at the mercy of the trainer and/or groom's dictating what is best, sometimes going against what their common sense or inner voice tells them. I've seen it over and over again and it's often the horse that suffers.

Aside from the money you'll save by caring for your horse yourself, think of the peace of mind you'll feel when you've acquired the knowledge to be the expert. When the vet or farrier visits you'll be able to tell them exactly what your horse has been up to lately. If your horse is a bit fresh when you go about a ride you'll know why. If he's off of his feed one day, you'll have a good idea what's going on. If he lies down at an unusual time of day you'll take note and perhaps prevent a colic. What would you give for such expertise?

For years I've wanted to write a book on the subject of caring for your horse yourself. Even when I didn't know I did it was always in the back of my mind every time I witnessed a situation that I knew could be handled better. After awhile my clients started suggesting I write such a book but I resisted thinking of all the work of trying to organize my thoughts, because I had held so much in my mind regarding horses for so many years. I finally started an educational website dedicated to the care of one's horse experience: *http://www.backyardhorseman.com*, where I address a large collection of equestrian topics. After a couple of years it came to me one day that my book on horse care was right in front of me, starring me in the face from my computer screen and so ***Horse Cents - A Sensible Guide for the Equestrian Enthusiast*** was born!

I would like to say that ***Horse Cents*** is a complete guide to horse care, but it is not. In fact there is no book or video or course of study that is complete, because caring for a horse is not an exact science. It's constantly evolving as we continue to learn more and more of what makes a horse the unique individual that he is. Instead ***Horse Cents*** is more of an introduction, a cheering section to urge you forward, letting you know I understand your dreams and your drive because I've lived it. By writing this book, I hope to inspire you and empower you to know you can do this; while peppering my counsel with extreme caution to not take any of this too casually, always keeping in mind that you are making yourself responsible for a noble creature's well being. Think of ***Horse Cents*** as your resource regarding the most typical questions surrounding your horse experience. Drop by my website to see updated information keeping you on top of the latest developments on horse care and stay tuned... there are more books to come!

GETTING STARTED

Are You Ready To Own Your Own Horse?

Do You Have The Time To Own A Horse?

Being Your Horse's Primary Caregiver

Fear Can Be Your Friend

Planning Your Own Facility

Thinking Outside The Box (Stall)

Can I Keep My Horse Alone?

You're Gonna Get Dirty!

ARE YOU READY TO OWN YOUR OWN HORSE?

7 Easy Questions Every Potential Horse Owner Should Ask Themselves.

Just as the kid from long ago that would press their face up against the pet shop window, you frequent the shows, watch the programs, take the lessons and do everything else imaginable to get that "horse" fix. You've decided now is the time to take the plunge and own a horse of your own. Before you do, allow yourself just a minute and ponder some of the questions and suggestions listed below to assess how ready you are to take on such a responsibility.

    1. Look at your finances! Talk about a "buzz" kill. Let me be frank, horses are a "high maintenance" pet. They require a small fortune to keep properly and even if you've brokered some kind of a "deal" with a friend or with someone who owns property, you cannot be guaranteed you will always have such an option. Be realistic about what it will cost you not only for now but further down the road in a number of years. Also keep in mind, there's no such thing as a "free" horse. Many times people are given horses (that should be a clue as to their expense) but even a free horse has to eat and be cared for and before you know it that "free" horse is costing you a cool grand per month not counting the unexpected such as those late night visits from your vet. How's that for free?

    2. What are your goals? Asking yourself what your plans are for your horse will also determine what his expenses will amount to. If you plan on competing then of course you will need training for both you and your horse and there's also the question of to what level you plan on taking this competition? Will you compete in the ranks at the community level where fun and positive interaction should always be a top priority (remember at this level if your trainer isn't fun as well as informative then find a trainer that is)? Or, are you planning on going into the big leagues which is another mindset, one that should not be taken lightly because this industry can be serious business? What's the difference you ask? Well, being conservative it amounts to about an extra three grand per month per horse. Are you into that?

    3. How stable are you? This could be a play on words couldn't it? Owning a horse is a life changing commitment. A horse doesn't live quite as long as a parrot but far longer than a dog or many other pets you may own. I had a pony live in excellent health until a stroke hit her at the ripe old age of 37! Do you have the resources and desire to accommodate that? And don't think you can always sell a horse or even give it away because that idea presents a whole other set of circumstances to worry about and cause you to lose sleep at night.

12

4. Where will you keep him? Here we go into the money again. There are some places in this country that are more suitable to horses in that they provide the space a horse needs to be a horse. I had a prominent vet from New Mexico tell me one time that he thought it criminal to keep a horse in a space any smaller than 5,000 acres! I understand not all of us have that luxury, "duh," but you do have a responsibility to provide as much room for a horse as possible and always with a shelter of some sort. If you must keep your horse within a stall, (preferably the biggest one possible), then you want to be sure that your horse has daily access to some kind of safe, bigger space to stretch and kick up his heels for as much time as possible. Remember, horses are herd animals and to be healthy they need to move as their body dictates!

5. How much time do you have? Time equates to money, so if you don't have the time and expertise you better have the money to pay someone who does! Again, I will state, (because it cannot be said too many times), horses are a "high maintenance" pet! They require countless hours of care and maintenance, often each and EVERY day! If you choose to own a horse you are responsible to that living, breathing creature; one who values moving as much as it does air to breathe or water to drink and that often takes time!

6. Can you love unconditionally? I assure you there's nothing better than a great experience with your horse but can you handle those times when things aren't working so well? When a bad day with your horse could result in an injury? Can you remain kind, loving and caring seeking the best in yourself as well as in your mount? Can you be firm and focused as well as rewarding with compassion and gentleness? Granted these virtues are worth developing, but not at the expense of an innocent animal that only reacts to those things put upon him. Please dig deep into your psyche and examine the true reasons why you yearn for such a responsibility. If it is because you crave the opportunity to control something then look to some other vehicle, because you can never truly control a horse. You can only influence him and gain his trust and respect. What you think is control for the moment can result in a disaster in the future.

7. How much do you know about horses? Be very honest with yourself. Those rides you went on thirty years ago when you were a kid away at summer camp do not qualify as experience! I understand the desire for horse ownership, but you must be realistic about how much you know. If you're anything less than a professional, then seek out someone you can trust to teach you correctly and keep you safe. Learn as much as you can before you buy a horse; even seek out opportunities to lease a horse for as long as necessary to learn enough to be a responsible horse owner/expert, because such a magnificent and noble animal deserves nothing less!

DO YOU HAVE THE TIME TO OWN A HORSE?

A really unfair question because if most horse owners took a realistic look at their time the answer of course would be "no." The truth is that owning a horse has to be important enough to you that you make the time. It's like anything else; if you care about your horse you'll find a way to be with him no matter what. If it helps to justify that allotment of time by looking at all the benefits then by all means do so. Think of the physical exercise, the mental clarity of the meditation aspect of the sport and all of the fresh air and interaction with that special creature only a few generations removed from its instinctive past.

If you're like a lot of horse owners you don't need to think of all the reasons for owning a horse. For many of us it was never an option, we simply had to have horses in our lives but unfortunately some people forget the profound responsibility that owning or being responsible for a horse brings. There are also those that although they see their horse somewhat regularly they're always in a hurry, they race in, race out, a few pats on the head, some treats and in a puff of smoke (or dust, as is usual) they're back down the road and away. I'm really not sure which is more grievous, those that come through in a flash or those that stay around long enough to attempt a quick ride? They hurry and brush the horse, tack up and scatter around to meet their time restraints. Soon as they're done with the short ride they hurry and untack and throw the horse back into his stall wondering where on earth the fire is?

One of the biggest mistakes these people make is grooming and tacking up their horse in a hurry. Because of their "herd" instincts, horses aren't too big on the brushing part to begin with. Grooming a horse is a ritual that should be done in a calm, methodical and thoughtful manner, one that portrays your interest in the horse itself and his wellbeing. Anything short of that and you'll miss out on a most important bonding experience. Rushing around to groom and tack up can be an annoyance for your horse but can also lead to anxiety on his behalf not to mention making mindless mistakes that only eat up your time at best.

The bottom line is if you've chosen to take on the responsibility of owning a horse you'd better do right by that animal and find the time to spend with him. Just like with anything, you get out of the experience whatever you're willing to put into it. If in looking back at what your track record of attention has been to this point and you're not impressed with it, it's not too late.

Make a commitment today that you will do better and find the quality and quantity time to relish that rare and wonderful privilege of calling an equine yours. In doing so, you'll find that your horse won't be the only one who benefits!

BEING YOUR HORSE'S PRIMARY CAREGIVER

If you were given the golden opportunity to be in charge of your horse's care would you know what to do to keep his life healthy, happy and thriving? Until you can answer this question with a resounding "YES" don't even begin to entertain the possibility, because you will have the responsibility of caring for a living being whose well being can demand a great deal from those who would look after them.

If the answer to this question is "NO" which is typical of most horse enthusiasts, you don't have to stop dreaming the dream of someday being in complete control over how your horse is cared for. Believe me, I understand that you, as the owner, know more than anyone what your horse's needs may be, (that's if you've spent sufficient time getting to know him). Below is a checklist of things you may want to consider before deciding if you have the right stuff:

1. Do you have the time? As a professional trainer for over 25 years, I would estimate that for each horse in personal care, you should plan on devoting no less than 3 hours per day in total. Horses must be fed at least twice daily (just as in people, smaller meals more frequently is ideal so you can add lunch or snacks as well). The stall or paddock must be cleaned (if shavings are involved within a "box" stall, for example, plan on tripling your effort and time spent). And horses must be groomed daily (in their natural environment, horses spend a great deal of time grooming themselves and one another). Besides, having ample time in a turn out each day, a horse that does not have access to a large area of land needs to be exercised. A simple ride can involve at least one and a half hours of your time. Multiply that by at least 5 times per week and you have a conservative estimate of what the overall amount of time invested, not counting the addition of visits from the vet, the regular sessions with the farrier, meeting the feed delivery, etc... look like.

2. Do you have the knowledge? Can you quickly detect a horse on the verge of colic? (It's the #1 killer among horses.) Do you know how to worm your horse and how often? Can you bandage a leg or place a tendon boot on your horse's leg properly? (If a boot or bandage is put on the leg in the wrong way it can cripple your horse, so much for protection or therapy.) Do you know what to feed your horse? (The wrong diet can lead to more maladies than you can imagine with everything from colic to tendon injuries many being linked directly to improper nutrition.)

3. Do you have the facility? More importantly do you have the space? Horses need room to move. They are herd animals and derive their sense of well being by moving at their discretion. Is the area well fenced, free of any

16

dangerous obstacle with shelter against the elements and with ample access to a good water source? Is it free of any noxious weeds or other organic hazards such as deep holes or protruding rocks or sharp tree branches? Do you have a safe place to store your hay and feed keeping it free from any moisture? Many people can find training facilities that make themselves available to the individual for boarding, but much of what's been listed above still applies.

4. Do you know how to properly clean your horse's stall? If a stall isn't kept clean your horse will suffer! It's a known fact that your horse can develop health problems from a dirty stall such as thrush in its feet (a bacterial infection that can be tough to treat and can render a horse lame), to excess worms (this can result from horses eating around their manure), to bed sores from not having their sleeping and rolling space properly bedded and last but certainly not least, flies! Flies can be a horse's worse nightmare biting and causing allergic reactions and horrible infections in their eyes. Flies just love manure and urine filled areas which provide them with the perfect breeding ground. The list seems endless over something as simple as cleaning your stall, yet there's no greater satisfaction than leaving the barn with fork in hand knowing you've provided a healthy living environment for your friend. It is instant gratification at its best!

5. Do you keep an equestrian first aid kit handy and know how to use its various components? Let's take something as simple as Bute or Banamine. Do you have the proper equipment and the skills necessary to "pill" a horse or administer a paste? It could save his life! Do you know how to poultice a leg or a foot to draw out infection? Can you properly give a horse an injection staying within the "safety zone" to prevent paralysis or even death? Don't think you'll never have to face such an issue? I guarantee you there will come a time for something such as the above mentioned.

6. Do you have an "expert" resource? Someone you trust that has you and your horse's best interest at heart to help you with what you may not know or expect to have to deal with? Choose someone that's kind and caring with as much practical experience as possible that doesn't mind babysitting you with your colicky horse at 2am.

7. Do you have a sound back up plan? What if there's a loved one that needs your attention living clear across the country. Who will come take care of your horse if you have to leave? Don't wait until it happens to figure it out. Have a firm plan already in place. Do you have an evacuation plan in case of a fire? Living in Southern California it is always a consideration and it brings great peace of mind knowing you have somewhere to evacuate to and a way to get there preferably with a professional hauler that knows what they're doing even in a panic.

I can think of few things as gratifying as caring for your own horse. They give us such a special companionship that few other animals can provide. Be sure to never take them or their needs for granted and always take seriously their trust in us to care for their well being and safety.

Caring for such a large animal is a huge responsibility that carries with it a great deal of expense both in our time, our money and our emotions; but should you choose to take it on, and if you do it to the best of your ability, you will never regret the experience for it is greatly rewarding and most likely will become a lifestyle that will last a lifetime.

FEAR CAN BE YOUR FRIEND

I doubt that's what you would be thinking when finding yourself sitting atop a fire breathing equine that's about to consider a spin out on a steep mountain cliff, or when you're approaching a three foot jump for the first time.

Healthy fear can save you from something you'd rather avoid. It's your internal guidance system and should never be ignored. It could be telling you that you need to perhaps take a step back or retrace your steps to be more confident. You need only experience something successfully enough times to bring you to a place of assurance and comfort.

If you had a friend that knew you very well and cautioned you regarding any subject you would listen to him, right? So why when that voice speaks to us from within we label it as cowardly and are encouraged to turn away from its promptings? How many times have I witnessed a trainer belittling a rider because of their fear? It makes me sad to think that trainer has missed a perfect teaching opportunity.

I believe in keeping a student within their comfort zone and giving them enough time to progress naturally. All things will come easily with enjoyable effort and time, often sooner than if the rider is pushed with fear to accomplish a goal.

Of course the potential for getting hurt is part of the process and beneficial to spurring the student to stay more focused and more willing to learn. It's hard to teach a person who has no respect for the power that moves underneath them. Healthy respect for the horse causes a student to work more diligently on their balance and proper position, the effective use of their aids along with greater mental concentration. My best students have been those with the most fear! It's something you want to embrace. It's what will catapult you to becoming the rider you've always dreamed of being.

There are those that don't know enough about horses to be fearful. Ignorance is bliss; but only until it causes you or your horse or someone else irreparable harm. Students who have no fear progress slowly in their training. They are careless and inattentive. They are unteachable because they think they know it all. Before I take on a new student they must go through an evaluation with me on a horse. They think it's for me to measure their skills, their potential; but what it's for is for me to determine their willingness to learn and fear is the greatest denominator.

If you have fear while dealing with your horse you need to listen to what it's telling you. Do you need the help of a professional? Does your horse need training? Often it's the rider that's giving the horse mixed signals to the point of frustration on both rider and mount's part. When horses get out of balance they will respond by acting up or if a rider is unsure about anything

19

the horse will sense your lack of confidence and take control of the situation often doing the opposite of what he's being asked.

The next time you experience fear you must stop what you're doing and take the time to figure out what it's telling you. Being with your horse should bring you pleasure and thrilling excitement not mind numbing, paralyzing fear. Seek out help from someone you trust and respect. Ride only with those that understand the rules. Be in the company of sensible horse people. Find a community of enthusiasts that have vast experience. Such advice seems daunting, but it's out there. You must start from where you are and keep your eyes open to opportunities to be around such people. It can take time to find such outlets but they're out there.

PLANNING YOUR OWN FACILITY

What's Necessary And What's A Luxury?

First you must realize horses don't care much about how fancy their living arrangements appear, but there are a few things needed in a facility that can make their life healthier and happier. You may want to glance down the list to see if there's anything you've forgotten to plan for.

    1. Horse's need space. There are many components to a successful living environment for a horse and space is definitely at the top of the list. Please keep in mind; horses are "herd" animals meaning they move! They were built to move, their well being, not just physically but mentally, depends on it! If you are to "pen" up a horse within the confines of a stall, by all means keep their time in to a minimum (ideally only at night and feeding time). His day time hours need to be out in the sun (with a shelter) and lots of fresh air with room to run.

    2. Horse's need ample access to fresh water at ALL times. I can't stress this enough. Do you know what a vet checks for first when he's out on a "colic" call? He'll walk over to see if the horse has water! Seems simple enough in this day and age of plumbing and automatic waterers; but hold on, I believe they have yet to invent an automatic waterer that doesn't break usually at a time when it's needed most, say at around 2pm when it's 108 degrees. The ideal situation is for your horse to not only have the automatic but a large bucket of some type (that he can't overturn) filled with fresh water. I can guarantee that you'll have far fewer incidents of colic along with other digestion problems, as well as a shinier coat and healthier hoofs. Yes, water is that important!

    3. Don't underestimate the importance of shelter. You can argue that in the wild horses stand out in the full sun, but the truth is that a horse seeks shelter under a tree or bush any time it begins to get heated and should have the same advantage under your care. A proper shelter also shields the horse from flies and protects his skin from the harmful effects of the sun. It's so important that counties, such as Los Angeles, will issue a citation if a shelter is not provided for each and every horse.

    4. Fresh air is a necessity. If you're planning to build a structural barn then you must be sure that its design offers a flow of fresh air adequate enough to divert smells and the effects of ammonia from urine soaked stalls. I assure you, try as you might, and no matter how well you clean, there will always be some smells from urine, especially in stalls cleaned only once per day. In no time, a closed up box stall's air can be stifling and to think we cage such marvelous beasts up in such conditions.

5. Is your feed protected from the elements? This problem can be a nightmare and you can lose a fortune from moldy hay not to mention vet bills from visits because of colic caused by bad hay. You need a weather protected shelter of some sort that still has lots of ventilation to house your feed, because hay MUST be kept dry. The slightest bit of moisture and your horses are at terrible risk if they're hungry enough to eat the toxic hay. Not to mention protection from rodents and critters that will contaminate your feed.

6. Is your fencing and stalls or corrals safe and secure? If there's any possible way a horse can get hurt where they're housed, they'll find it. I have known horses discovered in the morning with severe injuries and the reason was never found. You must thoroughly go over their living area with a fine tooth comb to at least minimize the risk. Also your gates must be securely latched, but even then I have known horses to be the reincarnation of Houdini and be able to actually open a latch, (it's amazing what their lips are capable of, I have seen it for myself). If you have an escape artist, adding a chain or clip to their gate is necessary to keep them safely tucked in their stall. Be sure to assess ahead of time what can happen if a horse does get out, (believe me it will happen at some point), that he cannot get hurt on what's out in the surrounding area, including getting into your hay and grain storage.

7. Do you ride on proper footing? If you plan to have an arena and round pen you need to pay careful attention to the footing. There are experts out there that specialize in providing the best possible ingredients for a recipe of success for whatever type of work with your horse you plan on doing. Different disciplines require different types of footing whether it's washed plaster sand, DG or one of the higher tech mixtures. I would recommend you talk with someone who seems to have figured out what works best for their style of riding and then get a referral for who to go to for the job. The wrong footing, bad footing or no footing can result in a cavalcade of injuries ranging anywhere from tendon and suspensory injuries to founder and even back problems. I can't emphasize enough the importance of proper footing. It can make or break your program.

8. In your layout have you provided for plenty of room in which to work? Before you cast your design in stone (or wood, brick, metal) you want to be sure you've taken into consideration what your daily routine will be. Have you planned for an arena? Whether it's a regulation size Dressage court or a roping arena you'll want to know what adequate or required dimensions are necessary. If you feel like you don't need a specified area to ride, because you only ride trails, I must caution you by saying there will always come a time that your horses may need to work out too many days off or those extra lunches the new guy keeps feeding, "cowboying up" is not what it's cracked up to be and the last place you want your horse to decide to exercise its energy by exhibiting "airs above the ground" is somewhere out in the middle of nowhere. Allowing your horse to have a little go in the round pen or arena before your ride could possible save you, and him, from a disaster.

9. Always keep safety in mind. From everything such as securing gates to designating traffic flow to parking, always keep safety foremost in mind; not only for the horses but for the people, as well. Play out in your mind every possible scenario to bring to light what steps can be taken now to insure the lowest risk or hazard. Spending a little time and great thought now will yield far greater benefit later.

Building your own facility is an enormous, but very satisfying, undertaking. Who better than you know what it is that will serve your horses and their comfort best? It's a wonderful thing to create a working environment to be exactly as you would have it, just be sure you are well aware of what it is you want and need and don't forget to enjoy it!

5 Reasons Why You Don't Want to Condemn Your Horse to Solitary Confinement.

I believe in the "Golden Rule" and not just for people but for animals as well. Before you put your horse away and back into that box stall ask yourself, "is that where I would want to live?" "What would I do in there for the next 24 hours with nothing to occupy my mind, but my food for a couple of hours and then what?"

Is it any wonder why "stable vices" develop? Just the mere labeling of them tells us that these bad habits are acquired through countless hours of boredom mixed with anxiety, sometimes fear, and that "climbing the walls" feeling that becomes their "normal" experience.

Often we treat our hardened and dangerous criminals with more regard giving them ample time to exercise physically, as well as opportunities to stimulate their minds. How much more important to an animal connected closely to its instinct for freedom would these avenues be, and why would we want to resort to imprisoning something that we supposedly love, knowing full well how the circumstances of imprisonment can rob them of a life well lived?

If the concern for your horse's psyche isn't enough to convince you there's a better way, then take a moment to view the list below for other reasons why you should consider a better address for your horse.

1. A horse's physical structure was created to always be in motion. Through millenniums a horse has evolved not just to move but to move fast. Their bodies have developed to extend across vast territories at tremendous and constant speeds. This is what their physical bodies crave and one of the properties they require to instill within them a connection to their existence.

2. Horses are "herd" animals. Again, since their origins, horses glean their security from being part of a "herd." This is their safety net; this situation allows them to sleep at night in peace, awaken in joy and gives them the security they require to eat their meals in peace knowing a predator cannot infiltrate the herd. Take this away by locking a horse up within bars or worse, where they have no one else to stand by them for protection and you destroy their world.

3. Horses are social. Horses crave social interaction. It's instinctive for a horse to want to bond with another. They are born with the desire to connect with other horses. You show me a solitary horse and I'll show you a horse on the verge of a nervous breakdown. It's as though the Great Spirit created horses as one of a whole and without that closeness of community, they are cut off from their stream of wellbeing.

4. Horses deserve fresh air and clean footing. Plenty of space and being free to find where they know instinctively is healthiest for them to live is a horse's God given inheritance. Who are we to come between that? A horse knows what is best for them and they on their own will gravitate to clean and comfortable surroundings.

5. Horses need mental stimulation. There are some who think a horse is a stupid animal, but I know quite a few that can easily outsmart their humans. I myself have been at the receiving end of a horse's intellect and it can often times not only be superior to many other species, but they have the additional benefit of their highly tuned sensory abilities. I'd challenge you to know when your friends are driving toward you for a visit while still miles away? I have seen horses react to their owners approach while they are still down the road in their vehicles far from site or sound. Take that level of intelligence found in a horse and lock them up with no input or stimulation; how can anyone be so cruel?

Look, I know there are numerous reasons to keep a horse in a box stall but always consider your horse's quality of life asking yourself if the price paid is too great? I urge you to seek other options and if there are none then take whatever steps necessary to insure your horse gets to spend plenty of time in a turn out with fresh air, sunshine and lots of company until you can arrange to make other plans. Your horse's mental and emotional health depends on it!

CAN I KEEP MY HORSE ALONE?

Absolutely NOT! Horses are "herd" animals. Everything that is needed for them to experience safety and comfort is found within the herd's social structure. Isolate a horse and you'll literally drive him crazy with stress and anxiety causing him to lose all self confidence, making him insecure and causing him to be nervous about everything.

Sounds pretty serious and it is! Keeping a horse to himself is one of the cruelest things you could do to them. Even bad company for a horse is better than no company; but please understand I don't expect your horse to share a stall, or even a paddock, because there are risks involved with horses being together in smaller spaces; but by all means have your horse somewhere where he can see, hear, smell and perhaps even touch another because without this he will go mad.

I suppose there's always some exception to this rule out there, but in all the years I've been around horses, I haven't found one. I've only seen those poor creatures subjected to the depravity of being denied something that its instincts have required since the beginning; weaving and cribbing as a result of their attempts to pacify their need for company. It's so sad and guaranteed to break your heart.

Now that I've convinced you of the importance of a horse having a companion, I must point out a few things that should be considered. If your horse is stabled with only one friend then you must be careful taking them away from each other. Be prepared for your horse, or the other, to act up. Try pacifying the one left behind with a bit of hay or something to distract him so they don't incessantly call out to one another working themselves into a tether.

Make it a common practice to separate them for brief periods so they, like a little child, will learn that the other will return. Build their time apart up gradually and never let them be apart long enough for one of them to stop drinking their water due to anxiousness. Unsoothed nerves in a horse can cause them to not only become dehydrated, but colic leading to a costly vet visit or worse.

Of course, having several horses together near enough that they can be social is ideal, but being able to see another horse only from a far off pasture doesn't quite qualify. In some cases it only makes the horse that's left alone worse, for he yearns desperately to have a companion. He can't help it, it's in his DNA!

Besides being with other horses, some equines enjoy interactions with other animals, as well, and can become attached to a goat, chicken or dog; but none of these are a replacement for him knowing he's not the only horse on the planet. The longer he's all alone, the worse his neurosis will get, leading him to lifelong stable vices that can never be fixed even when another horse does come into the picture.

So please, I'm pleading with you, never under any circumstance plan to keep a horse all alone and to himself. It's just not kind, nor fair, nor right. Be aware of your horse's needs and give him what God had created him to have, a friend!

YOU'RE GONNA GET DIRTY!

If you're thinking you can be your horse's caretaker and stay clean in the process think again. I'm reminded of that Thelwell cartoon showing a kid in their riding habit looking quite neat and tidy standing next to a very dirty and disheveled pony with a bucket and various bath and grooming tools sitting on the ground between them. In the next picture the pony stands perfectly gleaming all clean and shiny and the kid stands as a complete mess; hair everywhere, shirt pulled out of his breeches, dirt and soap stains amongst the once dandy attire now tattered and filthy. In my mind, that is one of the truest portrayals of horse keeping I've ever seen, so if you have any phobia's regarding dirt, dust, hair, sweat, grime, mud and other things I dare not mention for fear you are reading this while eating lunch, then you better find another passion!

I'm not saying you can't have some kind of "horse" interaction while avoiding these less than appealing conditions, but your experience will have to be restricted to simply having a groom hand the reins of your horse to you all tack up and ready to go for your ride. In actuality, there are probably more people out there where this is the case instead of those who like to be almost completely responsible for their horse's wellbeing. In fact many trainers earn a portion of their income by convincing owners they couldn't possibly be capable of caring for their horse themselves. It is typical for a training package to include a hefty up charge of hundreds of dollars to pay for grooming and care services and is greatly to the trainer's advantage for them to perpetuate the myth that only they know what's best for your horse. I believe in following such a practice for the sake of added revenue, those trainers are doing the horse owner a harsh disservice.

A complete equestrian experience revolves around every aspect of your horse's daily routine. It is the interaction from the ground that bonds a rider to their horse and vice-versa. In fact, it can be so satisfying and rewarding that many regard it as the very best part of being around their horse even to the point that they would gladly forgo the riding aspect of the sport altogether.

There was a time when I would read a bio of a famous groom such as Sandi Patterson with Big Ben and could not relate. I didn't understand what complete satisfaction one could have with a horse from the ground only, but now that I've experienced it for myself I totally "get it" and can appreciate her devotion and connection to that horse even more so than that of its rider.

I think the bottom line is to be prepared to roll up your sleeves and put a little elbow grease into your efforts. Even if your horse's care is supposedly provided by your barn or training package, be more "hands on" and get yourself involved with his day-to-day regiment. Boot him up, turn him out, clean his bucket, groom him, bathe him, well... you get the point. Try to make every effort to be the one that attends to him and you'll be surprised what benefits it will bring not only to your interaction with him but with all others in your life as well. That which you work and sacrifice for you will love!

THE BASICS

BACKYARD BISTRO: FEEDING GUIDELINES

The average horse requires around 16 lbs of hay per day, but the operative word is "average." Like people, some horses gain or lose weight easier than others and many variables exist. Whether your horse is known as an "easy keeper" or not often depends on his breed (a Thoroughbred will have a higher metabolism than a Quarter Horse). You also need to take into consideration the current condition of the horse, the weather (horses burn more calories in winter trying to stay warm) and the amount of work the horse is asked to do.

My point is, don't count on feeding your horse the same amount from day to day. If you are aware enough of his regiment you'll be better able to make a daily assessment regarding how much your horse needs for his feeding. Also, you'll want to break up the amount of hay fed for the day in as many feedings as is practical. If you can feed lunch to your horse it is beneficial to the horse on many levels both physically and mentally because horses were designed to eat throughout the day and throughout the night.

If you're having trouble regulating your horse's rations you may want to invest the time and energy into weighing out your hay per each feeding for as long as it takes until you have a better idea of what is most appropriate for your horse. Different hays and different cuttings present varying weights and what an average flake weights with the hay you have currently may change with your next shipment. Remember, horses do best on hay they can "graze" on (Timothy, Orchard grass, Bermuda and other grasses) with grain hays and Alfalfa fed in cautious moderation.

The bottom line is to stay flexible and be prepared to adjust your horse's rations depending on what he tells you by his condition. Stay on top of his feeding routine even if you think you have it figured out. A horse's needs change and you wouldn't want to miss the opportunity to keep him at the peak of health!

CLEAN YOUR STALL IN 3 SIMPLE STEPS

The benefit of cleaning stalls is one of the best kept secrets out there. I consider it a complete exercise in well being; one that not only provides ample opportunity for reflection or meditation but gives your body a much needed workout while being in the outdoors amongst some very good company. I have to laugh to think of how much one would pay to find such a class offered at the local gym or some posh spa in a vacation paradise.

Besides the health benefits of being responsible for a well kept stall, you receive the satisfaction of seeing your horse's stall turn from disgusting to divine knowing that you are responsible for the transformation. By spending what I consider the best ten or fifteen minutes of the day with your horse cleaning his stall, you get to daily assess your horse and his condition and state of mind. We often look elsewhere for, and spend good money to find, that personal connection to our horse when it's right there in front of our face.

Now that I've convinced you that cleaning your horse's stall is a task worth pursuing let me share a few hints that can prepare you to have the most rewarding stall cleaning experience.

First, I find it easiest to clean the stall just after the horse has been given his breakfast. He's calm and busy enjoying his meal. You can count on him staying in the same place long enough for you to do a bang up job on the stall without stressing about him walking through the piles or bolting out the door (although there are those rascals that head for the door anyway).

Next, have the tools you prefer. All manure forks were not created equal and over the years I've come to the conclusion that the best fork just happens to be the fork that you like using. There are all kinds: metal, plastic, bent, straight, etc. You just have to try a few to find your favorite and the same goes for the type of wheelbarrow or cart that you prefer. Everyone's different so find the tools that work best for you!

Use plenty of bedding. You can have too much but it's hard. Ample bedding lets you feel that your horse is comfortable and well cared for. For those horses in box stalls it's also protection from getting cast. Bedding in a box stall should be banked up high against the walls to keep your horse from rolling too close to the wall and getting stuck. It happens all the time and can have disastrous results, so put plenty of bedding on your list.

Set the mood. I like to play some good music. Note: Horses don't like hard rock, they'll tolerate pop or talk radio and they rather like smooth jazz but I hate to admit they LOVE country. Don't ask me how I know this; just trust me on this one. Don't wear anything you have to worry about getting dirty and allow yourself enough time to enjoy the moment. Now that we've set the stage let's get started!

Step 1. Start with the obvious. First pick up what's easily exposed. Just with that alone things are looking better already. Talk about "instant gratification!"

Step 2. Dig out the wet spots. It's great to get the urine smell out of there besides the moisture breeds bacteria.

Step 3. Search for buried treasure. I think this is the best part. When I do this I feel like a kid again out on an Easter egg hunt! It's amazing to think what you can find buried beneath shavings when you go looking; and as you do, you keep sifting over your dug out wet spot filling it in with cleaned shavings and Voila! Before you know it you're done! How easy was that?

I love cleaning stalls! When can you do such a good thing for yourself while you're doing something so good for your horse? Like I said, "the best kept secret." Don't tell anyone!

TO BLANKET OR NOT TO BLANKET?

Some Things To Think About Before You Open That Package.

So it's that time of year again. Next weekend temps will be back up but just for now we've hit a cold front that brings us rain and we're thinking of winter and what we can do to keep our horses comfortable. Before you consider starting a blanketing regiment, run down our list of questions and suggestions to insure you'll be doing what's best for your horse.

First you must ask yourself, "Why am I putting a blanket on my horse?" You may think the answer is obvious but with closer examination the answer may not be as evident. Often we blanket our horses to make "us" feel better because we can't understand how our horse could be perfectly comfortable in the worse climatic conditions; but they are, with some exceptions, and that we'll discuss.

Make an assessment of your horse's lifestyle and living conditions to determine what type of blanket is needed or whether he needs one at all? What does your horse do for a living? Is your horse a hard working athlete and will he be sporting the latest style of trace clip or full body clip? If the answer is "yes" then you will need to blanket and may even need two different weights, a light weight for day and heavier one for night. If your horse is one of those casual freewheeling types that keeps his winter coat and gets to lounge in pasture and only go out for an occasional trail ride then you may have other options. Take into account what kind of shelter he has to determine his needs. If he has plenty of room to roam and no shelter then he may be better off with no blanket because nature provides a horse with a defense against the cold and wet by trapping air under the hair. A blanket, especially one that isn't water repellant, will only compress the nap of the hair and actually cause your horse to be colder than he would be without it. Also, there are few blankets designed to not rub against a horse if they include a lot of movement around the pasture in their daily routine.

Does your horse live in a barn? If he doesn't have an outside run that allows him to stand out in the rain and get drenched he may only need what's termed as a stable blanket. These are not water proof therefore they breathe a bit easier and are often more lightweight causing them to be more comfortable. You must use caution to not over blanket your horse because he will get warmer in a box stall and could actually overheat which is far worse than being too cold.

~Do's and Don'ts of Blanketing~

Never expect a day sheet to do the job of a blanket! If I had a nickel for every time I've seen a horse somewhere shivering in the cold or God forbid the rain because they had on only a day sheet… again, a horse stays warm naturally by fluffing up their hair, trapping air in between that insulates the horse's skin from the cold making them quite toasty. Using anything that flattens down the hair and you're doing serious damage to your horse's ability to stay warm!

It is healthier for a horse to be without a blanket than wearing a blanket that makes them too hot! Horses can get very sick, usually due to colic, by wearing a blanket that is too heavy for their climate. If you're not sure then don't do it! Living in Southern California my horses rarely wear anything heavier than a lightweight blanket and even that comes off in the morning unless daytime temps are expected to not come out of the 50's.

Once you start you can't stop until the seasons over. So many people out there are too casual about their blanketing. They'll start putting them on after a few cold nights and then stop sometimes because it has warmed back up or just because they don't feel like doing it or have forgotten to. This makes me crazy! YOU CAN'T DO THAT TO YOUR HORSE! It is so unfair! There are a few exceptions like here in Southern California when the Santa Ana's blow and the thermometer doesn't drop below 70 at night. If you're sure it'll be warm ALL night then fine, but you'd better be sure. Remember your horse is better off without than with and getting too hot. To make an accurate assessment of the overnight temps go out to the barn around an hour before day light when it's most likely to be the coldest, check your horse's comfort level and then decide how cold it is.

You must wait in the evening until its cool enough to blanket. I hate certain times of the year such as early in the season when it often doesn't cool off enough to blanket until quite late. Too many people, for the sake of convenience, put those blankets on in the afternoon so they can hurry and go home. If you're lucky your horse will survive but think of his misery. We're always so worried they'll get too cold when we should worry about them getting too hot.

Know how to properly attach the blanket. Again people would think this would be obvious but most likely they're the ones that don't know a blanket's straps often crisscross behind the legs and under the barrel. I've seen horses at best be found the next morning all twisted up in their blankets because they weren't strapped properly; but at worst I've seen horses seriously injured because they got tangled up in their blanket's straps, panicked and hurt themselves. *DO NOT PUT ON A BLANKET UNLESS*

SOMEONE WITH EXPERIENCE CAN SHOW YOU HOW because there's almost a 100% chance you'll do it wrong!

Never, but never, work a horse in a blanket or trailer them in one! Horses put out a tremendous amount of heat just standing there. Trap that heat in a blanket around a moving horse and you're heading for a disaster! Especially with trailering, people fear the horse will chill from the wind in a trailer or want to keep the horse clean for a show and those are the same people that can't understand why their horse colics every time he comes out of a trailer.

These are just a few things you need to be aware of before you commit to a blanket routine. It is as with all things equestrian, if you introduce some element that is "unnatural" to your experience then you are bound to complicate matters that can compromise your horse's safety and comfort. Just remember to *THINK BEFORE YOU ACT!* Be aware anytime you are dealing with your horse. Remember "we" are their stewards. We have taken on a huge responsibility for their care. Do not do it recklessly or with no regard to their needs as a high maintenance pet. With sensible contemplation make the right choice and enjoy this winter!

YOU CAN BECOME A HORSE WHISPERER!

With One Simple Step...

Starting with the definition that "horse whispering" is simply speaking the horse's language you can understand that it's not hard, complicated or anything you cannot accomplish. It does become easier with practice when the techniques become more of a habit or instinct, but you can start the process the very next time you bring your horse out to ride.

So you wonder, what is this great secret? Well, I'll give you a hint... it's something anyone can do but many pass up the opportunity to influence their horse to their benefit each time they ride because they either don't want to take the time and trouble, it's a service provided for them or they've been convinced by their trainer that they're not capable of doing it for themselves. Are you getting a clearer picture of what I might be talking about? You guessed it... Grooming!

Sounds too easy right? If it's so important why does my trainer discourage me from doing it? There are several reasons. Sometimes a trainer is just too lazy to go through the process of teaching their student to properly and effectively groom their horse. (It's far easier to have the grooms have the horse ready and waiting in the cross ties, that way they don't have to worry about the student's lesson starting on time.) Also, most training programs charge extra for grooming so they don't want to be out the revenue. (If you groom your own horse, they don't make the extra money.) Then there's those trainers that feel a paid worker does a more thorough job of grooming and they don't want to have to nag a student about leaving a saddle mark on the horse, etc. (Of all the reasons, I can understand this one the most), but I'm convinced that the biggest reason a trainer doesn't have the student groom for themselves is because they don't know how good it is for your relationship with your horse. They simply don't understand the significance of grooming a horse beyond the actual task, so let me explain it to you.

It has to do with "herd mentality" (horse whispering). To begin with, you probably know that the head mare (alpha mare) actually controls the herd and the social interactions amongst them all. It has been discovered that one way she accomplishes this is by grooming. That's right. When a horse grooms another horse it places them in dominance over the other similar to other species such as monkeys. Are you starting to get the picture? When you kindly groom your horse, it's as if you are saying to it, "I'm in control. I'll take care of you. Your well being is important to me." See, it's not that horses have to be in control. They just want to be safe and if you cannot take control, they will take it for themselves to be secure. Can you begin to see the implications of this concept in reference to your riding?

If you start the contact with your horse from the ground, which is something even a beginner can master, then the experience of you being in charge transfers over to your riding and your horse will become a more willing partner.

Don't be fooled into believing you cannot groom for yourself. Ask your trainer if he or she will formulate a program to teach you to do this and be willing to pay them for their time. Many riding schools have classes where they teach special courses and believe me, it costs good money. You're not doing the trainer or school any favors expecting them to do this teaching for nothing.

So I challenge you to try this. Get some experience behind you and make a commitment to groom and tack up your horse personally. Of course many of us lose control of our schedules from time to time and it's great if someone at the barn is designated to do this for you on those occasions, but remember each time you do practice this easy and enjoyable regiment you will be richly rewarded. You will connect better to your horse, be more aware of him and his body and he will look to you with more confidence in your role of being in charge. How can you say no to that?

WHY DOES MY HORSE HATE BEING BRUSHED?

The 3 Most Common Reasons This Occurs.

Some horses love being groomed. They'll stand for what seems like countless hours while you primp and polish every inch of their body. They close their eyes and lower their heads as though they're enjoying every minute of their "spa" time. Then there are the others. The ones that weave and jerk and nip, swishing their tails and stomping their feet in obvious distress. Are they ill mannered or just foul tempered? No! Absolutely not! There are reasons horses don't like to be groomed. Read on to see if one of these explanations doesn't resonate with your own experience?

    1. Horses are sensitive. Some are just downright ticklish and the stroking of stiff bristles from a brush can send them into convulsions. If you don't believe me wear a pair of shorts the next time you're at the barn and take your body brush and scrape it against your skin. It hurts! It's been proven that typical methods of brushing a horse can be very irritating to them even causing their heart and respiration rates to elevate because of the stress of the discomfort. What can you do? Try using a soft rubber curry instead of a stiff brush to loosen dirt and hair then remove what appears with either a soft brush or a grooming rag. Your horse will be so much happier and will actually enjoy your session.

    2. Is your horse an Alpha? We must get into the dynamics of the "herd" mentality for this one, (horse whispering). You're probably aware that in the horse world there is a social ranking with one horse being dominant over another. Studies have shown that one of the ways a horse establishes its dominance over the other is to groom them. What a concept, the leader servicing those lesser, Congress are you listening?! I digress... If your horse has an "alpha" personality they will not want you to groom them because they feel it will undermine their position socially. This can be tricky to remedy and I suggest you work with some in hand ground exercises to build a bridge between you and the horse so she (it's usually a mare thing) can learn to trust and respect you. It takes a little time but patience can serve you very well.

    3. Do you have static electricity in the air? Certain locations and climates are more susceptible to this than others. My training barn is located near the "high desert" of Southern California where we have what's known as the Santa Ana winds. These winds create a lot of electricity in the air that transfers to the brushes against a horse's hair, also in the clipper blades and in their blankets and day sheets. I have had clients brushing their horses only to have them jumping and flinching and upon further inspection have found their horse's erratic behavior was due to the electricity in the brushes actually shocking them! A simple fix is to spray a fine mist of water across the brush from time to time or even pick up a can of Static Guard. You'd be surprised to see how much more dirt comes off of your horse leaving him looking much cleaner and shinier and "shock-free!"

So there you have it! That's pretty much it. These are only three possible reasons for your horse's behavior in regards to grooming. Next time you put your horse in the cross ties consider one of these possibilities.

THE IMPORTANCE OF PROPERLY FITTED TACK

Deciding exactly what saddle and bridle is appropriate for your discipline is hard enough (especially if you plan on showing), but you must also be just as certain regarding how well your equipment fits your horse. Unfortunately, this matter is often taken much too lightly with the most attention paid to simply how trendy or stylish something looks rather than whether it feels right to the horse or even the rider.

I'll admit there's quite a science to having one's tack properly fitted with volumes of books, DVDs and clinics featuring experts on the subject. Certainly I cannot scratch the surface of all that is needed to be known, but I can make an attempt to use this chapter to convince you of the importance of having your equipment properly fitted.

Let's start with the saddle. An ill fitting saddle can wreck havoc not only on a horse's back but their hocks, their shoulders and all the way down to their hooves. If a horse's back is sore from a saddle they will be unable to raise their back, bring their hindquarters under and drop their mouth onto the bit making connection impossible.

Just as with people, (actually even more so because a horse has to carry you on its back), when a horse's back hurts; everything hurts, and what used to be an enjoyable ride can become excruciating torture with the pain radiating throughout the horse's entire body. I once had a lesson horse that was sound but whenever a certain saddle was placed upon its back (even though it appeared to fit) the horse would step off lame at the trot every time. That little demonstration made a believer out of me as to the importance of the right saddle.

When a saddle doesn't fit the rider it can also hurt the horse. If a saddle's balance is off, making it difficult for the rider to maintain their proper position, the rider's balance is compromised causing them to inadvertently sit either ahead of the motion or behind it. This problem can affect every other part of the rider's body such as their shoulders, legs, hands and heels making them ineffective and even prohibit them from a connection with the horse. This can cause them to give their horse mixed signals by being unable to control their leg and rein aids. The wrong saddle can make even the best rider their horse's worst nightmare.

I suppose the same can be said about a bridle. If a bridle is made of hard, cheap leather or is the wrong size, shape or discipline style, it can be brutal on the horse or if it's not adjusted properly to the horse's head it can rub or pinch particularly around the ears and drive a horse mad. Imagine how you would feel if you felt like your head was strapped into a vice grip and we haven't even mentioned the agony that comes from an ill fitted bit.

Of course then there's the whole gambit of "other" equipment all with their unique characteristics where the fit is just as important. Martingales, breast collars and boots can yield disastrous results if their function doesn't match the need and if measurements don't add up.

There is one hard and fast rule that always rings true when it comes to buying properly fitting horse equipment... YOU GET WHAT YOU PAY FOR! It's true you can pay too much for some things, but it's important for you to become a smart consumer and realize that quality leather goods cost money. If properly cared for, your saddle or bridle can last a lifetime; at least of the horse.

Just as with a quality car, leather goods rise in value, as well, and you should consider its resale value when investing. I once bought my daughter a very good saddle and after ten years of daily use, we sold it for as much as we had paid for it. Now that's a bargain!

Keep in mind that some things are cheap for a reason. Most inexpensive tack can be ill fitting, feels horrible to the touch and will fall apart before you can soften it up with lots of elbow grease and product. There are some less expensive alternatives to leather, such as synthetics, but again, be careful because they're in a lower price range often they are manufactured with lesser standards so do your research.

I could be cold hearted and tell you simply if you can't afford quality equipment you have no business owning a horse and although there's a bit of truth in that statement, there are other ways to obtain what's best for you and your horse without spending unreasonable amounts of money. All over equestrian communities there are resale and consignment shops where you can buy used equipment. Doing so can be a bit tricky, but if you know enough to know the difference in the various "better" brands and you know what quality looks like, then you can save hundreds of dollars.

Never buy "used" equipment from someone that won't let you take it home and try it out on your horse. Any reputable dealer makes provisions for such things. There's a huge market in used saddles and even many retail stores take trade-ins. Going to places you trust to shop can make for a fun, bargain hunting outing especially when you're shopping with likeminded friends.

Remember when it comes to tack, if you're not sure of what you're doing seek the council of someone you trust and if your horse shows the slightest sign that you may have chosen poorly stop using what might be causing the problem and get some help to be sure you're not doing more damage. Just as with people, a back injury to a horse can cause him a life time of pain. Be sensible about this and not be in too big of a hurry to have the latest or what you think looks really cool. Keep what's most important in your mind and that is... how does it fit your horse? Does he move freely under it? Does he keep a low head and comfortable ears? If the answer is "no" to these questions then it doesn't matter how great or cool you think it looks. You must use what works, for you AND your horse!

TO BOOT OR NOT TO BOOT?

You're having fun shopping for the latest in equestrian footwear, so why not boots for your horse? Not so fast. I know there is some outstanding looking leg apparel for your four legged partner, styles that make your horse look like he's ready for action at Badminton or the Rolex but there are a few things you must be aware of before you slap that knarly looking equipment upon your equine transformer.

Just as with everything equestrian, be thoughtful and consider the functional properties of your equipment. When in doubt, I tend to be conservative feeling that "less is more" is the most prudent approach. Always trying to do what is most natural, I base my opinions on boots from a very practical standpoint and that is, you want your equipment to give the least amount of support and protection necessary to insure there is no infringement on the horse's development. When a horse's leg is exercised only within the confines of a boot I feel it can weaken the area and not allow it to strengthen to its fullest potential especially when the horse is young.

I'm not saying boots aren't a good idea, it's just I believe you want to be selective in their use. For example, say on a nice leisurely trail ride, when your horse's outings may be a bit more subdued, go "bootless" (In England, each horse is ridden out on the road daily before their workout, which is something you should be doing at least once a week to give your horse a bit of R and R, and doing it "bootless" is a nice way to build the strength in their legs).

Give some consideration as to the properties of your boots. An avid rider has a boot collection, a lesser boot for those simple hacks and only if the footing's a bit deep, something such as the Woof boot, a long time favorite for accomplished event rider Bruce Davidson, all the way up to something like the Eskadron boot you'll see in the show jumping ring. Personally, I steer away from the more solid boot like the latter mentioned because it's just way too much for my purposes. Remember to be conservative because you can do damage with a boot that's too restrictive and look for every "safe" opportunity for your horse to go without to allow for his muscles to feel the freedom of his ancestors.

Depending on your footing and your horse's energy level, boots for a turnout can be a must but again I caution you to keep it simple, and comfortable, offering just enough support to get the job done.

Boots worn for Cutting or Reining in Western training most often are in the back where the horse is trained to carry most of his weight as with Dressage, although for that discipline leg wraps are preferred which leads me to another subject... DO NOT USE BOOTS OR LEG WRAPS IF YOU DON'T UNDERSTAND PROPER APPLICATIONS AND FIT! You can do far more damage than good! If you put the boot on in the wrong direction you will be weakening or even damaging the leg rather than helping it stay strong! The same is more so with wrapping the leg! NEVER USE A STANDING WRAP FOR A WORKING WRAP AND VISA VERSA! If you don't know the differences then don't even think of using them! There are certain wraps for certain uses which are beyond the scope of this article. I don't want to scare you but there is so much to know on this subject that people spend countless hours perfecting their wrapping skills, so don't think you can master the technique of properly wrapping a horse's leg from one easy five minute tutorial on YouTube. I'm not saying you're not capable of doing an adequate job of wrapping, but only after expert instruction (in person) and hours of practice should you attempt to do so on your own.

I think the important thing to remember when considering boots or wraps for your horse is to keep things as simple as possible, that less is more and always consider function above style. Just as with everything involving your horse, you'll get what you pay for so be greatly concerned with quality and fit as it can help or hinder your horse's performance and overall soundness. The wrong boot or wrap or improper application can ruin your horse's legs, so tread cautiously and seek expert advice. And, when in doubt go without! I have a feeling you're going to thank me on this one.

DO YOU NEED TO PUT YOUR HORSE INTO TRAINING?

Key Questions Every Owner Should Ask Themselves.

Finding yourself with a horse and no ties to a professional is a difficult undertaking at best and often leads to anxiety that many equestrians are unprepared to deal with. It's gut wrenching to find oneself immersed into the grey area of wanting to do what's best for your horse but not knowing when or who to turn to. Hopefully the following suggestions can shed some light upon a task that without careful planning can produce what has the potential of becoming your worst nightmare.

Start by asking yourself what are your goals with your horse? How much time do you have available for your horse and how much you are willing or able to spend to secure someone with the experience you desire (keeping in mind, as with everything in this life, you get what you pay for)?

Your goals for your horse often depend on its breed and your experience. Although most breeds can be accomplished in many disciplines some horses (as with people) are better equipped for one style of riding over another and matching the horse to the task is very beneficial. For example, Quarter Horses for Western Pleasure or Warmbloods for Dressage. Next you must evaluate what you know about your chosen style of riding and whether it will conflict for what your horse is equipped to handle. Training a horse to go in a way that neither of you are comfortable or familiar with will do you both little good.

Make a realistic assessment of your time and willingness to be involved. While there are those who want the luxury of having their own horse to ride without doing any of the work in regards to their horse's care, there are many who want to be integrated into their horse's daily regimen. Be advised, you may have to go to great lengths to find a trainer willing to incorporate the owner into the training process, but they do exist. You just have to be undaunted in searching out such an individual.

Look carefully at your budget, keeping in mind some horses must stay in training an entire lifetime depending on what they will be expected to do, what their mentality is and what the owner's experience is. Even if you simply want a quiet mount to go on the occasional trail ride, some horses must see or experience something often or at least on a consistent basis to be relaxed and comfortable with what is being asked of them or where they may be asked to travel. Horses, like people, have a comfort zone and you need to be realistic about your abilities to see them through their challenges or whether it's best to have a professional deal with it.

How do I find the right trainer? Here's where networking comes in handy. Talk to everyone you know, trust, admire, respect… starting to get the idea? Ask someone whose horse is going in a way that you would appreciate. Don't know anyone? Go to your local tack shop or feed store. Find where groups that ride your discipline gather, be it a horse show, gymkhana, clinic or some other gathering. Talk, talk, talk, ask, ask and then ask some more, any and every question that comes to mind. Don't worry, people won't be annoyed. Horse people love to talk horse, give opinions and offer suggestions. Trust me, lend some horseman your ear sincerely and you'll have problems shutting them up. There's just one thing to keep in mind… let the ads you may come across be the last way you go about finding a trainer. There are exceptions but in my decades of experience a really good, kind and effective trainer seldom has to advertise. If you walk into someone's operation in response to an ad believe me when I tell you to keep your eyes and ears very wide open. Look for red flags and don't take anyone's word for anything. Be present as often as possible and if something doesn't make sense, call that trainer on it. I've had a simple philosophy that helps me weed out those that I consider undesirable, "if what's being done with your horse doesn't make sense to you it probably isn't making sense to the horse either."

Remember to keep your horse's best interest in mind. Think positive, expect the best, practice the "golden rule" and use the imagery of your horse at the end of the process being exactly what you desire and let that energy put you into a place that attracts not only the best trainer for your horse but for you as well. A good journey takes plenty of time. Enjoy the search and use the experience to learn more about yourself and your horse!

WHEN TO CALL OUT THE VET

There is much to learn about a horse's health and there are volumes of books on the subject so there's little I can do in one chapter to teach you about it, but I can emphasize how important it is to be aware and offer a few suggestions as to when your horse's symptoms signal a vet's visit may be in order.

Let me just say that you don't want to wait until there's an emergency to call your vet out for a first time visit. Seek a calm, easily scheduled excuse such as your horse's routine vaccinations or check up. Your vet can be you or your horse's best friend, so don't be shy about making an appointment for a ranch visit for you to become familiar with him and him with your horse. You don't want to wait until time is crucial and the clock is ticking because of an illness or injury to worry about giving him directions on how to find you or waiting until the office worker can get you into their data base. When he does come out have him explain to you how to run a baseline of your horse's resting vitals such as his pulse, respiratory rate and temperature so when there's a problem you can call him with the most accurate and up to date information, which will help him to assist you in your horse's care until he arrives. Also, vets can get held up with other emergencies so this information can help him assess how soon he needs to get to you.

Now that you're connected to a great vet and he knows you and your horse, the most beneficial advice I can give to you regarding when to call him is to first and foremost, know your horse! Know his schedule, his eating habits, drinking habits, napping, his attitude, his work ethic and overall general appearance. A sudden injury is obvious; that gash that might need some sutures, but would you know your horse well enough to notice whether he's suffering from colic symptoms or just having a nice bask in the sun? Could you detect the onset of founder before much damage is done to the foot? Do you know your horse's legs well enough to notice any undue swelling signaling a muscle strain, tear, bow or perhaps the signs of an abscess?

Horses love to eat so I would say your first symptom to look out for that would trigger a phone call to your vet would be your horse's appetite. Before you get crazed when this happens be sure to check his water supply. If a smart horse is thirsty he won't be eating because hay in a dry gut will surely cause some problems, but if he has plenty of water and your hay doesn't look contaminated in any way, and particularly if it's just at the onset of your horse's meal then those are good indications that he might be colicking and you'll want to take steps to further investigate because colic is the number one killer of horses. Other signs of colic are listlessness, your horse laying down, (or God forbid rolling which you should never allow him to do because he can then twist a gut which would require surgery), nipping at his sides or curling his upper lip. Instead of being listless your colicky horse might seem agitated, unable to stand still with a rapid respiratory rate. At your next wellness checkup have your vet show you how to listen for gut sounds so you can add this regiment to your list of indications to confirm your suspicions of colic. If your horse is experiencing any of these symptoms *call your vet immediately*! It may be a mild case and go away on its own but are you willing to take the risk? If you wait to contact him it may be too late and will require a trip to an equine hospital with expensive surgery that not only involves costs into the tens of thousands but great risk in recovery overall.

What if you came out to the barn one morning only to find your horse standing on just three feet? Let's say you've first checked the foot to be sure there's nothing in it, (my daughter's first Thoroughbred picked up a framing nail into a back foot only three weeks after we'd purchased him). If his limb is swollen and it seems to have developed overnight, his pain level is pretty severe and particularly if he's been standing in anything wet it might be an abscess. In time abscesses can eventually remedy themselves, but a vet can help speed the healing process along with keeping your horse from experiencing great pain not to mention correctly diagnosing the problem so you don't miss treatment on some other condition.

If your horse's leg appears to be swollen only at the tendon, thinking back to any physical strain your horse may have been under on the previous day can point you in the direction of suspecting a bow, tear or strain in the tendon or a ligament. This too should be addressed by your vet to obtain a proper treatment plan and garner an assessment of how long a recovery he needs to insure he avoids re-injury.

Your vet will also speed the recovery process by applying different bandaging applications. Unless you employ an expert professional (such as a groom or your trainer) be sure to get adequate training from someone qualified before you attempt to bandage your horse yourself. Not knowing how to bandage correctly can do more harm to your horse than good, so this is something you want to prepare for in advance in case such a skill is ever needed.

Of course there's the obvious cuts and scrapes (if there's the slightest chance your horse will need sutures then most definitely call out your vet), but sometimes it's hard to pin point such, as the time I had a large pony come up lame in a front leg. There was some heat but only a strange abrasion above his back heel. One would think scratches or a rub from an overreach boot but my wise and all knowing vet knew exactly what it was. He asked me if I had found the pony's lead rope clipped to the halter on his gate dangling in his stall. How did he know that? Sure enough, the pony had a nasty abrasion from wrapping his lead around his hoof and needed to be treated with antibiotics. Had I not called out our vet the poor pony would have gotten far worse before he got better.

So when you ask yourself, when is it time to call out a vet I suppose the answer could come in the form of another question and that is, "how well do you want to sleep at night?" Vet calls can be expensive but having peace of mind is worth a great deal. To save money, educate yourself so you're not frivolous with your veterinarian's time but when in doubt, call him out. I can guarantee you will never regret calling out your vet, you will only regret when you haven't.

SAFETY FIRST

Top Ten Things To Know That Could Save You Or Your Horse's Life

Seven Important Horse Safety Tips

The Dangers Of Leaving A Halter On Your Horse

The Dangers Of Riding Without A Helmet

The Dangers Of Riding Without Safety Stirrups

Poisonous Plants

First Aid Kit Essentials

TOP TEN THINGS TO KNOW THAT COULD SAVE YOU OR YOUR HORSE'S LIFE

I'm not sure you can be too safe or too careful when it comes to dealing with horses. Yes, I know you want to be able to gallop freely across a meadow or along a strand of sand but don't let your passion for the sport cloud your judgment about your safety. If you take a few simple precautions you can relax and confidently enjoy your horse knowing you've done your best at averting certain disaster.

1. Wear a helmet! You have two arms and two legs but only ONE head so don't take the chance of simply being lucky. Do the smart thing and set a good example by wearing your helmet. I did a little survey and just amongst a few of my equestrian friends, each and every one of them had a story of survival thanks to the fact that a helmet was on their head! That includes ME, when a brief little hack turned into a complete nightmare and had I not thought to wear my helmet I would not be writing this today.

2. Learn and use a quick release tie! If you don't know how to tie a quick release knot you need to find someone to teach you. I cannot count how many times this technique has saved a horse from certain disaster. If you think you know horses, but don't know about this, you cannot call yourself a horseman. It's that important!

3. Always ride in safety stirrups! It's hard to believe how many trainers risk their student's safety because they don't like the look of a safety stirrup! GET OVER IT! I blame the judges and the entire equestrian industry for not making such a ruling mandatory for any age. It's just ignorant and foolish to risk your life riding in a conventional stirrup. In today's market there are numerous variations on the traditional safety stirrup, so look into it and choose what can save your life. (Note: My Great Grandfather was dragged to his death by a horse.)

4. Never leave the halter on an unattended horse! I have another article on this extolling the dangers of such a practice. The article talks about a lovely horse of mine given to a little girl that loved him dearly and of his tragic death simply due to the fact that her Mother left the halter on the little girl's beloved mount. It is so needless and stupid. I don't feel any circumstances justifies the practice, just don't do it!

5. Never tie your horse to something that can break! You would not believe the things I've seen people tie their horses to, (present company included). From heavy metal stall sliding doors to the proverbial chain link fence. I think I've seen just about everything come loose when challenged by a thousand pound animal hell bent on becoming free. I even know of a Thoroughbred that single-handedly snapped a telephone pole sunk down into ten feet of concrete right off at the base and proceed to run around a ranch at top speed. You really need to be quite discerning regarding what your horse is being tied to. Doing so could save your horse from a terrifying experience, one that can scar him for life.

6. Secure your grain storage. Never store your grains or special feeds where a horse might obtain access to them! Look, I don't care how secure you think your horse is in his stall, whether your horse is an escape artist or you have an absent minded person leave a gate open, there will always be the occasional midnight madness when a horse manages to get out of his habitation and run amuck through the barn area. Such flights of fancy are guaranteed to culminate at the feed area where unsecure cans of grain can be easily accessed. Often when a horse overeats something quite rich it sets up a metabolic inflammation that can result in a serious case of either founder or colic or both. Don't take such a needless risk. Keep your special feeds in cans strapped down securely enough that if overturned your horse cannot spill its contents or better yet, keep your feeds safely locked away in a room that a horse cannot enter.

7. Wear a cell phone. If you must ride when no one's around be sure to have easy access to a cell phone and if you're like me and hate to be interrupted simply turn down the ringer but still keep it handy. And especially if you go out on a trail ride make sure someone in the group is carrying a phone. It's such an easy thing to do and could someday save you or your horse's life. Last year I was out trail riding with a friend and came across someone (by himself) that had been thrown by his horse resulting in a broken back. Where would he have been without a cell phone?

8. Tell a friend if you're heading out alone. This is the number one rule of hiking. Why should it be any different if you're riding? First off I don't like recommending anyone riding the trails alone, (there's just too many things out there that you have no control over) but if you must, make sure someone, anyone, knows that you're out there. Even if you have a cell phone on you make sure there's someone back at the ranch aware that you've gone out.

9. Know what the poisonous plants in your area look like. Here's a good argument for keeping a horse well fed but there are still horses out there that don't possess the sense of knowing what's good for them and what's not. Be sure to know how to spot what's unsafe for your horse to eat and take an occasional stroll around the paddocks and the pasture to make sure none of these harmful plants are present. Remember, just because he hasn't eaten it in the past doesn't mean for some reason he won't eat it today!

10. Wear a sturdy, close toed shoe! In our barn area no one is allowed in a shoe that isn't strong enough to protect the foot from a horse's hoof. There are absolutely no exceptions and no one rides in something that doesn't have enough of a heel or ankle support to keep a foot from slipping through the stirrup. Also there are no glass bottles of any kind allowed in the barn area for all the obvious reasons.

This is just a short list of some of the safety precautions you need to be aware of. There are countless more but these are some of the most important. Neglect to practice these principles of safety and I can guarantee that you will suffer the repercussions of your carelessness. It may not happen today or tomorrow but needless disasters will happen if you don't have the presence of mind to incorporate some of these safety standards.

Do you and your horse a favor and query yourself as to how many of these ideas are part of your daily equestrian experience. If they are not make them so, and breathe a sigh of relief knowing you've done your part in protecting that which you care so much about.

7 IMPORTANT HORSE SAFETY TIPS

Little Things You Won't Want To Ignore.

    1.   ALWAYS leave your horse's halter on the stall! Living here in Southern California, it's imperative that the halter and lead be left on each horse's stall because of the ever present threat of wildfires where it's sometimes necessary for total strangers, (firefighters and volunteers), to evacuate your horse where minutes or perhaps even seconds count.

    2.   NEVER leave your lunge line out in the arena or anywhere where the horse can reach it. If you turn your horse out in your arena or round pen, never leave the lunge line where the horse can get to it. I made the mistake of doing so more than twenty years ago discovering what I had done when I came down to the arena to put a sweet Quarter Horse away after a turnout. I found him literally hog tied with all four legs wrapped up together in a bunch. It was absolutely comical except for the disaster potential it possessed. Luckily, he was a very calm horse that didn't panic as I methodically proceeded to unwind the line. Any other horse that didn't possess his calm attitude could have turned this into a tragedy.

    3.   BE careful leaving a treat bucket in your horse's stall. We often leave a bucket of carrots or other supplements in the stall with the horse as we run off after a ride to our busy lives, but it's really quite dangerous as the horse can easily get its hoof stuck between the metal handle and the plastic. Play it safe, if you must leave something in there opt for a rubber flat feeding bowl.

    4.   BE careful feeding your horse its treat by hand. Before you know it you can train your horse to not only be a biter but he can become a complete nuisance constantly probing you and other things searching for a treat. Such behavior can wreck havoc upon your grooming routine and cause a simple tack up to take forever.

    5.   NEVER tie your horse to a stall door or anything that could pull out or break! I actually saw this happen once at a barn we stabled at. A horse, after being tied to the sliding box stall door, set back and in an instant pulled the door right off of its track and went running all over the ranch with a steel door dangling from his head taking out everything in their path, as well as banging up the poor horse's legs.

    6.   NEVER teach your horse he can open his own gate. We think it's really a cute behavior to have the horse push a gate open for us while we're on them. I used to think it was adorable too until my very determined Appy mare went to push the gate open to leave the arena and finding it latched pushed so hard that before I could pull her up she flattened the whole side of the arena pushing every bit of it down flat to the ground. Boy, did I feel stupid as she casually strolled across the mess to return to the barn.

7. NEVER leave the lead from the halter dangling in your horse's stall. This happened where one of my students didn't properly tie the lead to the halter on the stall in a way to keep it out of the pony's reach. The result was a horrible rope burn across the back of the pony's fetlock because he had pulled it in and got it caught around his ankle causing a nasty infection and a hefty vet call and antibiotics.

Of course this is not a complete list of all the little things we do that can get us into trouble, but it's a start with the point being that we just need to be more mindful of all the dangers out there no matter how trivial they may appear. Remember one hard and fast rule; if there's any possible way a horse can get hurt you can be sure he'll find it! Don't give him the chance!

THE DANGERS OF...
LEAVING A HALTER ON YOUR HORSE

So many times growing up around horses I remember a common warning was to never leave a nylon halter on a horse unattended. As I became a professional, I also issued the same warning to all of my students and any one handling a horse, because it did make sense but, in all honesty, I never thought the worst case scenario being, a horse breaking his neck, would ever actually happen. I mean really... have you ever known of such a thing? Well, I'm here now to tell you it does indeed happen and it happened to one of my best horses.

I'll have to go back many years and to a student that was all things horses. The girl practically lived at my ranch. Because of her fierce desire and dedication she became a competent rider; very quickly mastering in weeks and months what would take others years. She continued to improve being spurred on by the goal of someday riding a brilliant but complicated horse I owned that few people rode because he was almost too talented for his own body and mind and was often quite a handful. I put off her requests to ride him, for as long as I could, until finally, as she pleaded with me her case that she was ready, I gave in, telling her it was her funeral and to not be too disappointed if her ride ended badly. Much to my surprise, it did not, and that was the beginning of a beautiful relationship between a young girl and a horse that was her world.

The girl and the horse went on to do things nothing short of amazing, all along being the best of friends. They had great success in competition along with enjoyable trail rides and great fun at play days. It seemed there was nothing the two couldn't do well and I watched their bond grow until one day her beloved horse was the first in my barn to go down from having been poisoned with the infamous botulism outbreak in Southern California. It was finally detected that it came from the hay cube feed and ended up being responsible for many equestrian deaths.

With the vets not knowing what we were dealing with at the time, my instincts told me it had to be the feed and I changed the feeding regiment in time to save my entire barn with the exception of this one horse who steadily grew worse even though we had him plugged into an IV and we were doing everything we knew possible to save his life. I'll never forget the long, countless hours this girl sat next to this horse's near lifeless body, stroking his neck and whispering softly to him that he would be ok and she would always be there for him. This girl's dedication went beyond the boundaries of caring as she only left this horse's side when it was very late into the night and her Mother would insist on her coming home. And, as I would rise very

59

early to go out to the barn the next morning, she would already be there tending to him, dressing his huge gaping sores - a result of his body dying from the inside out.

The horse lived on the brink of death for over a week when finally one day the girl came into the house screaming that Alfie was up! He was up and wanting something to eat. None of us could believe it and as we all ran out to see that the horse was alive, the thought of how many times I tried to talk the girl out of spending so much time with him because I thought he would die was a blatant testimony to the power a girl can have with a special horse.

That was when I knew I had to give Alfie to her. I had to admit to myself that she loved the horse even more than I and proved herself worthy to care for such a fine animal. To me, he was just a nice horse, to her, he was her world. Even to this day, and in light of what I'm about to tell you, I have never regretted that decision.

Alfie's recovery took some time but the girl never tired caring for him and in time he was better than ever with the two of them again in the jumper competitions and winning at the regional level assuring them a spot to compete at the Arab Nationals that year in Scottsdale Arizona! It was after this accomplishment that Alfie came up with a lameness that was diagnosed as a pulled suspensory and would take a year of lay up to deal with. It was a great disappointment but the girl's dedication held firm and her family resolved to finding a quaint facility near their home where he could spend some quiet time healing.

It had been several months and Alfie was doing well with his leg healing fast. The girl's entire family embraced this horse because of what he meant to her and it was not uncommon for the girl's Mom to stop by in the evening, after work, to spend some time with him even though she knew her daughter had been with him much of the morning. It was on one such evening that when driving away from her visit the Mom realized she had left Alfie's halter on him after she had given him a good grooming. As she continued to drive toward her home, even though the thought of what I had taught her about the danger of leaving a halter on burned in her mind, she dismissed her worries telling herself that she was running late and that she had never heard of such a thing actually happening.

The next morning, as was usual, the girl was out to visit her horse even before the help had arrived to feed and to her horror she was the first to find her beloved horse laying there with his lifeless body dropped in a heap but with his head in the halter strung up, attached to a post he had sought out to rub against. Apparently, when he went to scratch an itch on his head the halter had caught over a post on the corral, he panicked, pulled back and broke his neck!

Can you imagine how the girl's Mother must have felt when finding out she was to blame for such a horrible thing happening to not only her daughter's horse but her best friend? And all because she had been thoughtless and paid no heed to her inner voice telling her to go back and take care of what she had left behind.

So my friends, here is my warning to you! NEVER but NEVER, **EVER** leave a halter on a horse unattended! If there is some situation that demands a halter be left on then it MUST be either made from leather or have a breakaway leather strap on it! Believe me when I tell you… if you leave a halter on a horse they will start to itch under it and they will find somewhere to scratch and chances are huge that they can easily slip it over something and get caught. Are you willing to take such a chance for no reason?

THE DANGERS OF...
RIDING WITHOUT A HELMET

I've known of far too many situations where someone was severely hurt by riding without the protection of a helmet, don't you? Yet it's taken a few years for me to finally get smart enough to realize what a silly and reckless thing it is to go without. Is keeping your hair nice or your head cool really worth risking a head injury often leading to a concussion, a coma or even death?

I can give you countless reports of such things happening each and every year! It doesn't matter how well trained you or your horse is. Things just happen. I've had ponies simply walking that tripped over a tree root and fell down dropping their rider to the ground. It's bound to happen sooner or later.

So why are we still seeing people riding without a helmet? Do they think it's cool? I'll tell you what's not cool and why I won't be caught without a helmet on my head anytime I'm on the back of a horse and that is I fear the ridicule I'd receive from my savvy and wise students if I ended up with a head injury because of neglecting to do something I am adamant about for them! Dealing with their disappointment in me would be far worse than any physical injury and I'm glad of their expectations because they keep me determined not to give in to discomfort or appearance!

As adults I feel we need to set the example. (You know the kids look at an adult without their helmet like they're the most stupid person on the planet and come on, do we really need to give them something to use to diminish ourselves in their eyes?)

Just logic and good sense tells you why you need to wear a helmet. As I say to my kids... "You have two of everything, two arms, two legs, two hands but only one head, if it breaks you have nothing else to take its place."

Today, more than ever, we have a huge variety of helmets with which to choose from, everything from super cool to super hot! There's a helmet for every discipline and every occasion and something that can fit into any budget.

No matter what you're riding, how you're riding or where you're riding to, you need to put on a helmet!

THE DANGERS OF...
RIDING WITHOUT A SAFETY STIRRUP

Many years ago I had a superintendent of a local school district call me knowing I was involved with kids and horses. Seemed his district had a school sponsored riding program and one of the little girls had in a lesson been dragged to death by the horse she was on. In horror I responded to the news with the question, "Why, had the safety stirrup not deployed releasing the girl's foot?" His response to my question was, "What's a safety stirrup?" I was shocked! And after explaining the necessity of such precautions, and sharing with him the realization of how senseless the little girl's death was, I warned him that he'd better hope that the parents didn't contact me regarding the tragedy because I would council them to go after the school district for blatant neglect and endangering children's lives. Maybe it's because my Great Grandfather was dragged to death by a horse, but I've always thought it reckless to be riding a horse without some type of safety stirrup. Although a typical Western stirrup offers a little more protection against losing one's foot, especially when wearing a Western boot, it's just careless to ride in an English stirrup without it being equipped to release if a rider gets their foot hung up through a fall, or is crazy enough to ride without a boot, such as in wearing a tennis shoe, which is courting disaster.

There are many types of quick release stirrups on the market ranging anywhere from the most common "peacock" stirrup to those on hinges and other designs that are more elaborate. They start at prices as reasonable as $30 to $40 and go up from there depending on how camouflaged you want the safety features. I think the point is, you can still be a slave to fashion and have the protection a safety stirrup offers, so vanity is no longer an excuse. All of my students use some sort of safety "quick release" stirrup as well as helmets no matter what their age. Why take the chance of going without? In my mind, it's just stupid!

My hope is that people will stop being ignorant about this and start realizing how important a simple safety feature can be and that I'll never witness again the sight of a little child being thrown from their pony only for it to be standing there at the jump still attached to the child by their foot hung up in the stirrup. As far as I'm concerned, it should be a requirement for any junior just as it is now for regulation helmets.

Wake up people and especially parents! Do the right thing and put you and your children into proper and safe equipment. Be determined to never ride again without those safety stirrups. I will guarantee there will be a time that you will be grateful you went to the expense and relative little effort!

POISONOUS PLANTS

A book on horse care would hardly be complete without a few words on toxic plants. While most well nourished horses just naturally steer away from eating things unhealthy there are those "Labradors" of the horse world that will devour anything they can get their teeth into so it's important to become familiar with the most common offenders and try to eradicate them from your horse's environment.

Below is a simple list that I encourage you, the reader, to research so you'll be more aware of what some of these poisonous plants might look like, where they are commonly found throughout the country, how each plant does its damage, what symptoms might occur and treatments available. I highly encourage you to do so particularly for those plants that grow in your region. However, I think it prudent in most cases to just avoid the plant altogether.

Alsike Clover: Short clover with blossoms. The entire plant is toxic and grows throughout the U.S. but best in places that have adequate rainfall. In time, continued consumption will cause liver disease.

Azaleas: Grown mostly as ornamental landscaping. Consumption of the leaves can kill a horse within a few days if left untreated.

Cherry: All varieties. The leaves (particularly when dried or withered) and even bark, produce cyanide and can kill a horse in minutes to hours.

Black Walnut Tree: Grows mainly in the eastern regions. It's not the consumption of the tree that can cause problems; it's the hooves coming into contact with the plant. If as little as 10% of your shavings in your horse's stall are Walnut your horse can likely experience a bout of laminitis so it's very important to know where your shavings are coming from.

Castor Bean: A large ornamental plant. We have a ton of it growing everywhere here in Southern California and even right outside our barn along the trails, it's lethal! All parts of the plant are toxic, but especially the seeds which contain the deadly poison ricin.

Deadly Nightshade: A plant related to the potato, tomato and pepper plant all of which are toxic to horses. It features growth to 2 to 3ft., delicate white blossoms and black and green berries. It likes dry, sandy soil and can be found growing wild almost everywhere. The entire plant is toxic and if enough is ingested it can cause death.

Horse Chestnut: A large tree common to the eastern coast and Canada and planted for landscapes now on the west coast. The tree is poisonous when it's growing. The young sprouts and leaves are toxic and can induce coma within hours.

Lupine: A spiky wildflower that grows throughout the U.S. It's a legume and depending on the species can actually be used as forage but only at certain times of the year. It's the seeds that are toxic and has little effect on a horse when eaten only once but if over time enough is consumed through being dried in hay or eaten fresh in a pasture it can cause a horse to suffer toxic hepatitis.

Milkweed: Grows wild in all parts of the country. It can be found in hay because it grows commonly around open fields. All parts of the plant are toxic, both fresh and dried, and it takes only a small amount to make a horse sick and in little time perhaps even cause death.

Oleander: A large flowering ornamental shrub that grows mainly in the Western and Southern states. All parts of this plant are deadly if eaten and often in only a matter of hours!

Poison Hemlock: A large fern type plant that can grow up to 6 feet. It grows wild in woodlands and around pastures. All parts of this plant are extremely toxic, both fresh and dried. The most common symptom of poisoning is finding the horse dead in the pasture because its effects are so quick.

Red Maple Tree: Grows wild in the Eastern states but used for landscaping throughout. The leaves are most toxic and if enough is ingested can cause death.

White Snake Root: A plant that grows between 2 to 3ft. with white flower clusters in the Midwestern and Eastern regions found in lush woodland areas or around crop lands. Effects can come from a large consumption of the plant at once or gradual amounts over time if found in pastures or hay. Symptoms occur over a period of a few days and death can occur if enough is consumed within 3 to as long as 14 days.

Yew: This is a small tree or shrub that grows up to 20 ft. in height. It features sharp appearing leaves and bright red flowers and berries. It's used widely in landscapes most commonly in the south and along coastlines. The entire plant is so toxic that as little as eight ounces consumed can cause death within 5 minutes. This happened to one of my clients who lost four of her beloved horses when a gardener threw the clippings of this tree over a fence and into the pasture. They found the horses dead with the leaves still in their mouths.

This by no means is a complete list of dangerous plants. I have only highlighted some of the worst offenders. I think the point here is to be more aware. Be aware of what is in your horse's pasture and even what is growing around it in case a wind blows leaves or components of poisonous plants into your pasture. Know where your hay comes from and absolutely NEVER feed your horse grass clippings because many of these plants are used in landscaping and can find themselves landing upon your lawn.

Lastly, know your horse and his usual behavior. Many symptoms of poisoning can start out subtle. Know your horse's eating and drinking routines, his sleep patterns and overall personality so you can be alerted at any change in his demeanor. Remember the faster you can get treatment to a horse where poison is suspected the better chance your horse may have of recovery.

FIRST AID KIT ESSENTIALS

I thought I should share with you what I feel comes in pretty handy when you're faced with an injury or illness of your horse. Of course there's no substitute for a vet's care, when needed, but even after a visit from him there are often a few things needed to keep your horse up and running.

If you're unfamiliar with these items or don't know how to use them, I counsel you to get some help from a professional because knowing how to treat your horse for various maladies can literally be a matter of life or death or at least soundness verses otherwise.

Listed below is what I consider the essentials. You may want to add to this list but remember to try to keep it simple so things don't get cluttered, costing you valuable time when seconds may matter.

Box of Large Sterile Gauze Squares: For placing medication on legs or hooves.

Package of Rolled Cotton: For bandages, wounds and hoof problems.

Package of Sheet Cottons: These come in handy to both dress a leg wound and as a sterile type of quilt to use in a bandage.

Package of Newborn Size Disposable Baby Diapers: Use to hold medication or a poultice securely onto a hoof.

At Least 2 Rolls of Vet Wrap/Co-flex: For bandaging legs and hooves.

Roll of Duct Tape: Great for bandaging a hoof or to serve as a quick easy boot.

Pair of Standing Bandages with Quilts: Always bandage the supporting leg!

Roll of Saran Wrap: Used in Furacin sweats for treating leg inflammation.

Medications: Bute (for inflammation), Banamine (for pain), Azium (antihistamine but also a steroid so be careful!)

Betadine Surgical Scrub: Absolute must have for cleaning a wound.

Vetericyn Wound & Infection Spray: Is a non-irritating, antibiotic-free rinse that doesn't cause skin or eye irritation. Great for flushing a minor cut, scrape or abrasion.

Vetericyn Ophthalmic Gel: Great for rinsing and treating irritated eyes. Provides relief from burning, stinging, itching, pollutants and other foreign materials (like dust & hay). It's steroid-free, antibiotic-free, non-toxic and speeds healing.

Neosporin First Aid Antibiotic Ointment with or without Pain Relief: Great for treating and protecting minor cuts, scrapes and abrasions. You can cover it with Alushield Spray Bandage to form a nice protective, yet breathable barrier.

Swat (clear): Is a great fly/insect repellent to use over minor cuts, scrapes and abrasions. I will often put Swat directly on top of Neosporin to keep flies and other insects away from a treated minor wound.

Ichthammol: Good for drawing out the infection of an abscess.

Alushield: Water resistant aerosol spray bandage.

Other Items: Rectal Thermometer, Vaseline, Scissors, New Sponges, Saline Solution, Rubbing Alcohol Wipes, Hand Sanitizer, Hand Soap, Rubber Gloves, Clean towels/washcloths.

To keep these items all in one place you'll want to choose a sturdy, lightweight container that's big enough to house all of your implements but small enough to throw in a trailer to take to a show or other venue. (There's nothing more gut wrenching than being away from home and needing something to patch your horse up).

With time there may be other items you feel would be good to have on hand but I urge every horse owner to have at the ready at least the things I've listed above and do whatever it takes to become proficient enough to understand how to use these items and know how they would serve you and your horse.

Like they say, "A pound of prevention..." Trust me when I tell you that there'll never come a time that you regret the money, effort and energy spent in preparing for what I guarantee at some point in your horse experience will surely come.

TRAINING PHILOSOPHIES

Are You A Rider Or A Passenger?

Horse Training 101

Prepare Your Horse

What Riding Discipline Is Right For You?

How To Find The Right Trainer

How To Build Your Horse's Self Esteem

When It Comes To Horses, There's No Down Time

Don't Put Your Horse In A Box

Are You A Chronic Round Pen Wrangler?

Rules Of The Trail

Why Dressage?

It's All About The Outside Rein

When Is My Horse Ready To Start Jumping?

How Important Is My Jumping Position?

Why Do I Need To Ride Different Horses To Be A Good Rider?

Using Your Voice As A Training Aid

ARE YOU A RIDER OR A PASSENGER?

Take This Quiz To See Which!

If you have to ask this question chances are fairly good that you're the latter, but just in case you're wondering you may want to take our quiz to be sure.

1. *Are there days when going through the "in" gate feels more like you're riding through the gauntlet?*
2. *When you ride on the rail do you feel like an Indy car driver being smashed into the wall?*
3. *Do the words "tally ho" cause you to grab on to the nearest piece of hair or anything within your reach?*
4. *Does throwing your body forward and grabbing onto something sound like a good strategy sometimes?*
5. *Can you feel your horse laughing from time to time?*
6. *Do you feel like your horse is on a tractor beam moving toward the horse in front of him?*
7. *Do you feel a strong impulse to have a glass of wine or other libation before each ride?*

If these questions seem silly to you then you may pass on reading the rest of this article. For the rest of you by all means, please continue.

1. *Do you know what it means to have your horse in front of your leg? I'm referring to impulsion and having your horse moving up into your hands for a "connection."*
2. *Do you understand the concept of an opening rein, a direct rein and the importance of your outside rein when it comes to your horse's balance?*
3. *Do you stop your horse with your hands or your seat? Hands (reins) are really quite ineffective compared to your seat.*
4. *Do you support your horse through its downward transitions? (Most people collapse in their position trying to stay soft but in doing so they cause their horse to lose its balance.)*
5. *Do you understand the importance of diagonals and leads and the role they play in your horse's balance?*

Most of those questions relate to your horse's balance and that would sum up the difference between you actually being a rider or just going along for the ride. If you can properly affect your horse's balance then "congratulations"

70

you may be well on your way, or perhaps have already arrived, when it comes to being a rider.

If you're not sure how to answer the last five questions and you don't like your answers to the first seven then you may want to consider getting some help in the form of training. For the greatest value I recommend a good Dressage trainer, someone whose ego isn't too big and teaches in terms you understand. If the trainer doesn't make sense, speaks in what seems like a foreign language or talks down to you, find a different trainer. It's not a matter of time spent on your horse that improves your skills. Without proper training, you will only continue to perpetuate and find new and bigger bad habits, often at your horse's expense. Time practicing proper instruction is the only way you can get to the point where you can consider yourself a "rider."

What doesn't kill us only makes us stronger. If you think I'm referring to the rider, you'd be wrong. I'm referring to the horse and will make an attempt to convince you that you can never win a battle with a horse. You may think you've won but instead your horse has won a golden opportunity to figure out your weaknesses, becoming more aware of his strengths and I assure you he'll plan on using them the next time the two of you meet. So you may wonder what you are to do. My advice is to find another way to deal with whatever it is that's not working. The biggest problem is your horse doesn't speak your language so you must find a way to bridge the gap and manage to communicate what it is you expect from your mount.

When schooling other people's horses often I find they have been giving their horse mixed signals usually from their body language exhibited by their riding position. Often it's as simple as a rider's hip angle. One such example was my neighbor who came to me one day asking to borrow a crop. Seems her new Andalusian mare only knew how to go backwards. I asked her to demonstrate. She was glad to oblige and I was a bit horrified as she leaned forward pulling on the reins and clicking and kicking the poor horse thinking that was the way to move forward.

I tried to contain my shock over what she was telling the horse and gently explained to her she only needed to open her hip angle, lean back just enough to put her position "behind the motion" and give to the rein with her hands. In a flash her horse jumped forward almost as though she was relieved to be allowed to do so, the poor mare. I felt so sorry for her and how she'd been trying, but her rider just didn't speak her language.

You can only imagine the nightmare I would have created if I'd loaned her the crop! So often when our horse doesn't respond in the way we expect, we react before thinking over what it is we may be doing wrong, and at the same time our horse is discovering our buttons so that the next time they've had it with us they know exactly how to get away with whatever it is they'd rather be doing.

I think the most valuable piece of advice I can give you the next time you're considering battling with your horse is to stop and think for a moment. I think the famous Chris Cox explains it best when he admits frustration from time to time. He says that frustration is his signal that he must be doing something wrong and he stops and doesn't proceed further until he figures out what that thing is. Imagine someone as horse savvy as him, recognizing that miscommunication can happen. How much more possible is it for us to be making some mistake?

Always come from a place of understanding with your horse. If you don't have that where you're currently at in your horse's training, then keep going back toward the beginning until you find it. Once you're at a place where you and your horse are on the same page, start building again. If you find yourself hitting a wall at some point and can't seem to get past it, then seek some professional help because the chance is great that it's you making some mistake. It will do you no good to continue to fight with your horse over something you're doing wrong.

Horses are quite willing to please us once they know what it is that we want. The least we can do is meet them half way. Having a solid education regarding a horse's language will help. There are many experts and methods out there to enable you to better communicate with your horse; you just have to find the one that works for you. Some of the better ones I've found, or at least the ones that resonate with me are anything Linda Tellington Jones or Buck Brannaman teaches, with Chris Cox, Clinton Anderson and Pat Parelli also making a great deal of sense. You can find their DVDs everywhere, but if you can get to one of their live clinics you're way ahead of the game. Just remember, there are NO bad horses, only bad riders!

PREPARE YOUR HORSE

It doesn't matter whether you're coursing at 4ft or heading out on a leisurely trail ride, without proper preparation you could face some serious setbacks. You can call it mindful horsemanship or "Zen" riding but from the paddock to the performance ring, following a methodical plan for getting your horse ready to work will eliminate wasted time, effort and energy not to mention possible injuries.

Let's start with the simplest exercise in horse work, the turn out. How hard can that be? Actually it seems more horses are hurt during a simple turn out than at any other time. To insure your horse's safety, first assess the turn out area. Is it safely fenced? Is the gate secure? Are there obstructions inside such as rocks, wire, loose fencing, etc...? Can the horse reach through the railings and make a meal out of the foliage growing next to the fence? Is the footing so deep your horse could pull a tendon? So hard that he could scrape his fetlocks or hocks from lying down to roll? Or is the footing so uneven that he might pull a suspensory? Did anyone leave any "equipment" in the turn out area such as a lunge whip, water bottle, lead rope, etc...? Do you have the proper tendon boots on your horse to protect his legs or bell boots in case he overreaches and scrapes his heal or pulls a shoe? Can he jump out and, if so, how dangerous or secure is the surrounding area?

So now that you're starting to get the idea, let's proceed. Let's talk about the round pen. Many of the same precautions above apply, but now you have a little more control. First thing you need to consider is that the horse will be going in a circle around you. Having a constant bend in a horse's frame puts a lot of torque on his legs and the faster he moves the more it pulls on the tendons and stresses the joints. Tendon boots are a good idea as well as taking it quite slowly when the horse begins. There's great danger in sending a horse out on a circle at higher speeds without giving him a substantial warm up. The truth is, it's dangerous at higher speeds, period and so a proper warm-up is crucial as well as exercising a good deal of restraint on the handler's part.

But you say you're just going on a little trail ride? What sort of preparations could possibly be needed for that? To start with... has your mount been out lately or is he all hot and anxious because he hasn't been exercised for some time? Depending on your horse, this is where a bit of a turnout might be on the agenda. It's not fair to expect him to be relaxed and attentive to you if he just needs to go out and rip for awhile. It will be a much more pleasurable ride for you and your horse when he's not dancing on needles underneath you while exhibiting maneuvers along the trail that even a Lipizzaner would envy.

74

If you're jumping your horse consider him an athlete taking all the precautions necessary for any sport using the proper equipment for his protection and comfort. Warm ups are essential as well as cool downs, taking breaks in between sessions so that he may avoid being winded. (Remember, when a horse is pushed past his ability to replace oxygen in his blood to nourish his muscles injuries will occur.) Your horse should also be warmed up gradually over smaller jumps before taking on something bigger. I so enjoyed watching Michael Matz once as he prepared for a Grand Prix competition by jumping mostly over a small 2ft vertical in the warm-up ring. His philosophy was that every horse only had so many "big" jumps available to him in his lifetime and that they should be used sparingly.

So you tell me you're only going to do a little Dressage? My question to you is, "are you going to ask your horse to go onto the bit?" Do you know that in doing so you're asking your horse to engage from behind which requires a good deal of muscle strength and control and it is unfair to expect your horse to do something that difficult without being properly warmed up. It would be comparable to a Yoga master doing a full lotus without first stretching, resulting in some seriously sore muscles the next morning or something worse like pulling a muscle or popping a joint, ouch!

I think whether you heed what you know is proper warm-up for your horse depends on how much he means to you and how well you appreciate his efforts. I can only imagine it is not easy to be a horse, especially when the owner either is ignorant of his horse's needs and the demands his requests put upon his horse's body, or the owner just doesn't care to take the time to insure his horse's comfort. It is hard enough for your horse to do what it is you want when all the conditions are right, so do your horse a favor and help him out a bit. Recognize him for the tremendous athlete he is and be determined to help him reach your goals in reasonable comfort and health!

WHAT RIDING DISCIPLINE IS RIGHT FOR YOU?

If You're Not Sure Whether You Should Ride English or Western, this Quick Quiz May Shed Some Light On Your Dilemma.

1. **Figure out where you want to go.** If you plan on riding mountainous trails then you'd better be in a Western saddle. English saddles can be more comfortable, but few offer the support and security when climbing difficult terrain. By the same token you wouldn't want to jump with a Western saddle because not only is it too confining for the horse to move in but the saddle horn can really get in your way, ouch!

2. **Determine what's best for your horse.** While almost every horse can do something of everything to a certain level, some breeds are more capable than others when it comes to the different disciplines. For example, Thoroughbreds for racing and jumping, Quarter Horses for Reining and Cutting, Warmbloods for Dressage and jumping. Don't get me wrong, there are jumping Quarter Horses, Dressage loving Thoroughbreds and I even knew a Western trail champion that was a very large Warmblood, but the point is, some breeds are more suitable to some disciplines and it's great to start with what is more likely to work.

3. **Assess your skills.** Although it can take as much skill to ride Western competitively as it does English, in the beginning, English is more involved with balance simply due to the size of the saddle and longer and stronger gaits from the horse. A full canter is always harder to stay within the beginning than an easy, soft lope.

4. **Figure out where you want to go.** Hey! Didn't I already ask you that question? No, this time I mean with your riding skills. What do you want to do with your riding and how serious are you about training? I have trained both English and Western, but I start everyone English because there's so much more we can do to assess and improve your balance and movement with the horse. You can take someone who's learned to ride well English, put them in a Western saddle and have them be quite successful in their riding but you can't take someone out of a Western saddle and expect them to be able keep a proper position in an English saddle. It just doesn't happen. So if you want to learn the most for the time and money invested, start with English!

5. **What feeds you emotionally?** I know it sounds rather "fluffy" to be talking about such things but stop and think for a moment what you picture in your mind when you think of riding. Do you see yourself on a ranch driving cattle to a pristine mountain pasture or jumping in a show to the thrill of the crowd or feeling the exquisite movements of lateral work from your

horse beneath you in a Dressage ring? To be practical, horses are far too expensive and time consuming for you not to be doing exactly what you want to do with them. There will be days that you'll feel challenged and it's those mental images of how you picture yourself engaged with your horse that will pull you through it.

Most importantly, regardless of what you decide, gain a firm understanding of your horse and get as broad an education in horse care and behavior as possible. Because no matter what discipline you ride, your communication starts and ends with it being just you and him. No Western, no English, just friends!

HOW TO FIND THE RIGHT TRAINER

Whether you're just getting started with horses or you've been around the horse world for some time, finding the right trainer can be a daunting task that can lead to heartache and regret if approached without caution. In an effort to sort through some of the confusion, we've listed various considerations along with answers to some burning questions. So relax, take a deep breath and let's get started.

The right trainer will: keep you safe, boost your confidence, use proper terminology, use formal techniques (i.e. lunge line, private instruction, etc.), teach you horse care and expect for you to have an active role in preparing your horse for the lesson. He or she will use kind and gentle methods for both horse and student, have happy, well cared for horses, stay focused and teach in a way that just makes sense.

WHERE WILL I FIND SUCH A TRAINER?

Ask everyone you know and certainly those whose horse and riding skills you wish to emulate, (don't worry about being an imposition with your queries; everyone loves to share their opinions).

Take your time and compare notes. Ask around the neighborhood, in feed and tack stores. Call your local equine veterinarians; they can be an excellent resource.

Even if you're a beginner, get yourself to a show exhibiting the style of riding you wish to pursue and watch in the warm-up ring for how the trainers there relate to their students, the horses and the craziness of a show. When you see someone you like, approach them for more information. (Remember, they may be super busy and their card is the most attention you should expect for the time being.) Later in the week, give them a call and set up a time to go out and simply observe one of their lessons. (Any reputable trainer would love to have you audit a session.) If you like what you see, book an evaluation. Do not commit to anything until you've actually had a lesson with the trainer, then you can make a more educated choice. If a trainer pressures you in any way, walk away because in my opinion even if s/he knows what s/he is doing s/he has hers/his priorities screwed up if s/he pressures you for anything!

Pay no attention to advertisements. Look, this is the way I see it... if s/he is a good trainer then they won't need to advertise. Even with a trainer that has relocated, a good trainer is seldom at a loss for clientele even in a new location because word often precedes them and they're booked up in no time.

The wrong trainer will: talk down to you making you feel small and insignificant, talk in such elaborate terminology that they get you totally confused and frustrated, lose their patience with you, talk big about themselves or do a lot of name dropping, let things distract them such as cell phones and other clients, sit on the rail barking out instruction, throw you in a group too large to get anything accomplished, have sour or ill cared for horses, use improperly fitted tack in ill repair, will pressure you to buy a package, isn't prompt or respectful of your time, doesn't give to you the attention you deserve or the worst, put you in dangerous situations.

WHERE DO I FIND A BAD TRAINER?

Most likely first from an ad. A bad trainer cannot hold onto clients so they're constantly looking for new ones to fill their schedule. Rather than letting their reputation stand for their abilities they list their services in various horse periodicals.

At shows, where they're too busy schmoozing with someone (usually with money) to notice a student needs help or is at the rail smoking nonstop looking upon the class like they know what is happening, when, in fact, they're clueless. Theirs are the students that often lose, much to the trainer's ridicule and condemnation.

At poorly maintained, run down facilities. Not that they can't be found anywhere, even at new, well developed barns, but chances are good that if it's a barn that is unkempt with little concern for the horse's safety and well being then it would only make sense that the trainer there shares such a mindset.

At parties because rather than do the work, they think the way to progress is to "network" and talk about themselves hoping someone will notice and take their word for things.

Hanging around anyone with money because they don't know it's really about other things such as horses being a vehicle with which to teach valuable life's lessons of unconditional love and belief in oneself and taking pride in accomplishment.

The bottom line is to be careful about choosing who you will entrust either with your horse or yourself. Be sure you know what it is you're looking for and what it is you want. Take the time; take all the time you need to decide. You have every right to ask questions and watch what's going on. I even have a friend who would spy on a potential trainer. She would watch undetected from a distance not only how he treated his horses and students but how he treated his help as well. I was so proud of her!

Whatever you do, don't go into a training situation blindfolded. It's wonderful to always think the best of someone but please note there is great abuse in the equestrian world, perhaps even more bad trainers than good. I'm not sure, but please be careful, choose wisely and if at any time you feel your trainer no longer serves you then do yourself a favor and look elsewhere. Just as you can't expect to stay with the same horse forever, (although if you're lucky it happens), you may come to a point where it's time to move onto another trainer. This is something you should face as a possibility from the beginning so you'll be better prepared if that is needed for you to progress.

Please don't underestimate the importance of having the right trainer! It's worth whatever effort you will go through. You won't be sorry you took the time! Good luck and happy hunting!

HOW TO BUILD YOUR HORSE'S SELF ESTEEM

Does it matter? Of course it does! Horses are just like people in that their self confidence and belief in who they are has everything to do with how they respond to us. Their self esteem will affect how much trust they have in us and how willing they are to do whatever it is we ask of them or even give to them.

Let me illustrate such a concept by telling of an experience I had recently with my neighbor's horses. She has two, both rescued. One was a lovely older Arabian whose owner passed away. She was very shy, timid, scared, fearful and hard to approach or put a halter on and had never been taught to go under saddle. The other was a young Pinto, national show horse with similar breeding but this horse was outgoing to the point of being gregarious, willing to follow and although quite rambunctious, anyone could sit on him. It was sad watching the Arab skulking around afraid of her own shadow but exhilarating to watch the Pinto; tail and head high prancing around as though he owned the place with a joyful demeanor, always up for a romp and with an attitude of excitement to meet each day.

What was the difference between the two? Self esteem! It was made clearly evident to me that day when I had an extra apple and thought I'd offer it to the Arab. (I've always been one to try to boost up the underdog.) I was surprised when she actually stepped over to me because she often stood quietly over in a corner under a tree and as far away as she could be from civilization. But, today, she made the leap of faith and came to see what I offered. I held the apple out as far as I could to get her near enough to it. She sniffed, baulked, blowed and sniffed again. This routine seemed to go on forever as I continued to coax and assure her it was edible and a good thing. Finally, just when it seemed she would get close enough to investigate, here came the Pinto bouncing gleefully over and without so much as a pause, all in one swoop, stepped right into her space and gulped up the apple; batted his eyes in passing, his way of saying a big "thank you," and went on about his business. I couldn't help but notice this life's lesson as I mused over the difference in the two of them and how we look at the world. As Dr. Wayne Dyer states in "The Power of Intention," we either look at this Universe as something to fear or as something good and for us to enjoy. To the Arabian, the apple was something to fear because she had poor self esteem and expected everything in her life to be a threat. To the Pinto, and without any investigation, he simply knew the apple had to be a good thing because it was coming from my hand and because of his high self esteem he knew he could trust me and expected everything in his life to be good. Can you begin to understand how this concept could have an effect on your horse's training? Which horse would you rather ride? Go to a show with? Go on a trail ride on? Jump? Rope a cow off of? So now you'll want to know how I get my horse to this place. How can I build his self esteem?

To be fair, it seems as if some horses are born more fearful and untrusting than others, but I'm thinking it's not so much their DNA as much as it is the imprinting of their Mother and/or their first early experiences with other members of their herd and especially humans! But there are still things you can do. First off, it has to be a mindset. You have to be determined to prove to your horse that his life is a good thing; that he can trust you, and life is not only fair but fun. You do this by always being kind to your horse and by knowing and speaking his language, and if you want him to trust you, you must never let him down. It is up to you, his human, and his herd leader, to earn his trust!

That being said, of course, you don't let him literally walk all over you. Remember the part about "speaking his language?" If you don't know about horse behavior or what people label as "horse whispering" you might want to study that for awhile and become more confident in your horse communication skills.

When you teach new concepts, and your horse is getting frustrated, don't hesitate to go back to something they can do well. Asking him to do something that's already in his repertoire and then praising and telling him how great he is can lift his spirits and bring back his focus. Come on, we do that for our other pets, do you think your horse is less intelligent than them?

I once worked with a Thoroughbred that was having issues, but if I took a break and went to doing awesome turns on the haunches (which he could do even at a canter) his mood lifted immediately. We made it a game and as he excelled at this very difficult maneuver I would shower him with endless praise and in no time we could go back to what he had found to be difficult and I would find little or no resistance whatsoever, almost as though he was a completely different horse and in a way he was.

So my advice to you when you hit a wall with your horse in his training is to find and go back to that one thing you know he can do well. Spend as much time on it as is fun for him and affords you the opportunity to convince him of his worth and then try your challenging work again. If the task is still too much for your horse to cope with then finish with something he can conqueror. Call it a day and assure him he's the greatest and you appreciate his efforts.

Remember, building self esteem takes time and patience; perhaps the lifetime of your horse, but I can assure you being more aware of his need to feel worthy can greatly change your attitude toward him and his toward you allowing him to not only feel safe and secure but willing to go the extra mile for you, causing you to be a more mindful rider and thoughtful trainer.

WHEN IT COMES TO HORSES, THERE'S NO DOWN TIME

I used to tell people this referring to green horses or those who needed to be reprogrammed, meaning that no matter what you were doing with the horse it was a learning experience; but one day I had a client put things into a more aware perspective.

She decided to amend my pearl of wisdom to include all horses all the time. It was instantly an epiphany moment for me when I realized she was right. Indeed, no matter who or what your horse is, YOU are teaching him something with every interaction. Whether you're working seriously in the arena, chatting with friends while holding your horse, getting tacked up in the cross ties, going into his stall to put his halter on or out for a leisurely trail ride, he is reading your intentions loud and clear (at least to him). Each day I see examples of this concept and I thought I'd go through a few to make my point...

Probably the most obvious is a horse that has been hand fed. When a horse is abrupt and nippy often pawing their hooves, tossing their head and rummaging their nose across a person, it's usually because they've been fed a treat from a hand. They can't help their behavior. They've been trained to think that with enough prodding their reward will be a sweet one. Unfortunately, it's these innocent creatures that get smacked in the face or worse as a reprimand. Now stop for a moment and ask yourself... what is this horse being taught? He's not going to associate your abuse with the search for a treat. He will however link such pain to your touch and then people wonder why their horse shies away from them.

A similar error can be when an owner always has a treat waiting for their horse when he returns to his stall. The result can sometimes be a horse exhibiting annoying behavior while in the cross ties, being led or gate sour when under saddle because the horse is impatiently awaiting that treat that comes at the end of his session. Again it's the horse that unfairly takes the brunt of the rider's frustration and wrath over something that can be solved with an easy change of routine.

Then there's the horse that has no respect for its handler's space. When being led it walks into the handler or God forbid steps on him. It's not the horse's fault and he's not being careless he's just responding to instinct. A horse will naturally crowd into your space; it's a "herd" thing. People often compound this problem. Being unaware, they invite the horse into their space with their body language by continually touching the horse (petting) under the guise of affection. A horse's instinctive response to this attention is to reciprocate with gestures that are inappropriate for a human's reception, causing another reason for the horse to be inappropriately punished as if he's doing something offensive. And so it goes...

The list of mistakes a handler/rider can make is too lengthy to post, but I'm thinking you get the idea. Just simple things we might do around our horse add up to become big behavioral problems and the truth is YOU are the one that's responsible. No matter what you do (or don't do) you are relaying a message to your horse and teaching him something about how you expect him to react to you.

Remember... there is no down time. Your interaction is always a teaching moment. Be sure of what it is he's learning from you and be doubly sure it is a message of love and understanding.

DON'T PUT YOUR HORSE IN A BOX

Beware of the trainer that treats every horse the same using the same techniques and labeling those that don't respond well as worthless or untrainable. Horses can be as diverse as and more complicated than people because, besides their intelligence (as people debate it exists), they also act upon their instincts which makes them often smarter than their handlers. The additional attribute of instinct that they bring to the equation can also bring to them a good deal of hardship and pain due to misunderstanding.

The above thought saddens me because of my move to another facility; I leave behind a complicated but good natured horse that must go onto another trainer simply due to its owner's distance and travel challenges. In a year's time this horse, that I'm very fond of, went from being a complete rogue to being a very talented and fun individual, but not without constant work on his balance and me thinking of various ways to keep his mind occupied.

It's not about running a horse into the ground to keep them in an agreeable state. With some horses, the more you work them, the more fit they become, and the stronger they are, the more horse you have to deal with. It can be a vicious cycle and if you're not careful to employ methods that occupy their brain, even more so than their body, you can produce a very fit monster.

Don't get me wrong. I appreciate a fit horse, as much as the next rider, but when it becomes more about the horse's inability to focus because they're so fresh, that's when you're facing a problem, especially when you're responsible for keeping a junior rider safe and competent on their mount.

So how do you keep a horse's head in the right place without having to run them into the ground? First, every horse is an individual. You have to invest the time to know who the horse is and how he best responds. It took me months to uncover the recipe for keeping the horse I'm speaking of on the planet and I do worry that the new trainer will simply treat him as an animal.

You must be open and flexible enough both in your time schedule and technique to move your horse along as "his" attention and focus allows, being careful not to progress at a pace that makes him anxious while keeping him from getting board. For many trainers, this can be a challenge because if a horse doesn't respond in the typical fashion or time allowed, the trainer's ego can get in the way and they can't deal with the fact that some horses take longer, or different methods, to learn just as with people.

Sadly what often happens in such cases is the trainer becomes frustrated and takes it out on the horse while labeling him unsuitable for the discipline or worse giving him the title of worthless and untrainable, (see chapter on *"The Disposable Horse"*). Just like people, every horse has their strengths and weaknesses. A good trainer will play upon this concept and through accentuating the positive traits build up a horse's self esteem, bringing him to a place of confidence and trust in his rider.

If you're not sure what your horse's training experience involves, or how he's being treated by the trainer, take the time to do some investigative work. Show up on those days when he's being schooled by the trainer and watch their interaction. Is your trainer relaxed and responding in a positive way to your horse? How is your horse responding to his/her instruction? Are his ears relaxed, eyes soft and jaw loose? Is he chewing and licking (a sign of acceptance and understanding) or are his lips pressed together tightly and pointed? Is his tail lifting softly in joy or is it swishing like a helicopter ready for takeoff? These are just a few clues to watch for if there are no obvious signs that there might be some discord between your horse and the trainer.

Remember, there's no point in your horse's achievements if he's unhappy. Your responsibility as his owner is giving to him the best life possible with happiness being at the top of the list. If you're convinced he isn't happy and secure you must take the steps necessary to remedy the situation. Consider a possible trainer change; not ruling out the barn environment can also be a deterrent to his wellbeing. You may have to look at a possible discipline change. Not all horses are happy jumping rails or racing barrels. Try to find what makes your horse the happiest and if you cannot give it to them, consider letting someone else do so.

The bottom line is to look closely at why you own a horse in the first place and let your desires be your guide. There are people (only a few) that pursue equestrianism merely as a sport and for them I am dreadfully sorry because they are missing the opportunity to realize that owning and working with a horse can provide so much more than a blue ribbon or a pay check. Find a trainer with great expertise, but is in it for the love of such a noble animal! You'll never regret it as you enjoy a very happy horse.

ARE YOU A CHRONIC ROUND PEN WRANGLER?

Questions Every Owner Should Ask Themselves Before Going Through The Gate.

So you've been enjoying the work you've been doing with your horse in the round pen. Never before has your horse been more focused and submissive. His balance has improved along with his temperament and you feel like you've finally reached a point where you have a connection. That's wonderful and I'm really happy for your sense of accomplishment however there are a few things you may want to consider and at what price you've realized your success.

First of all, ask yourself what does your horse's stress level appear to be during these sessions? Does your horse seem nervous and fearful? There is great wisdom in trying to reduce your horse's stress no matter what the training process is and running around chasing him like a mad man seldom offers your equine any sense of peace and stability. Understanding the typical "join up" methods can serve your purpose with a little modification to increase your horse's sense of self worth. Remember, just keep it simple and keep in mind you want to help your horse develop better self esteem. I know it sounds crazy but the horse that feels good about himself is much more willing to yield to your training requests no matter how challenging they may be.

Next, do you find yourself using the round pen as the most convenient form of exercise for your horse? While riding in an ample sized round pen could be experienced daily with benefits, caution must be taken when deciding how often to work your horse in the round pen without a rider to control his balance. (I gave you a hint with the word "balance.") Use extreme care with sending your horse in circles especially when he's free to be off balanced. When a horse moves in a circle or bend, particularly with speed, it causes significant amounts of torque to wreck havoc on his tendons, feet and all of his joints and once he's winded, LOOK OUT! You have a recipe for a disaster most often in the form of a bowed tendon or pulled suspensory, not to mention a myriad of other joint and muscle issues.

Have you adequate experience with round pen methods? Many people think working a horse in a round pen merely involves chasing him around and around until exhaustion. I can understand how this would seem to the untrained eye, but a master trainer has a lot going on between him and the horse and if you're using the round pen simply to wear your horse out you're missing a golden opportunity to greatly affect his mind, as well as his body. There are many self proclaimed "horse whisperers" that will be glad to take your money and profess an ability to teach you the various techniques. Some of these people do know what they're doing, but I admonish you to keep one thing in mind... ask yourself as you watch, (I have to pause here to point out if a trainer wants to work your horse only when you are not there then run for the corral gate with your horse and don't look back!) as I was saying, ask yourself, "does what this trainer is doing make sense to me?" I'll guarantee you one thing if it doesn't make sense to you; chances are great it doesn't make sense to your horse either! Get a new trainer that can explain EVERYTHING and have it make sense to YOU!

Last but not least, are you running your horse around in the round pen because you're afraid to ride him? It's fine to work your horse in the round pen a few minutes before each time you ride just to get a "read" on him and what his attitude may be for that day, or to make a mental connection, especially if the horse is young or just new to you; but you're doing yourself and your horse a great disservice by sending him around in circles all day because you're too afraid to be on his back or, God forbid, too lazy to tack him up and ride. While I understand fear and the massive hold it can have on some, if this is the case, why not take him for a walkabout (as the Aussies would say) or even put on some comfortable boots and take him out for a jog in hand? You'd be surprised what a nice long walk, complete with pleasant conversation about anything, can do for your friend, as well as for you!

Here's something to keep in mind, your horse is a living, breathing, noble creature with an active and inquisitive mind. They're just like us and can easily suffer from the boredom of sitting around in a stall all day just waiting for you to come over and do something fun with them. Does running around in a circle for an hour seem like a good time to you? The round pen serves a great purpose, but make sure it's not too much of a good thing. It can come back to haunt you!

RULES OF THE TRAIL

10 Common Sense Rules To Insure A Pleasant Ride.

When I take a group out on a trail ride, upon our return, people at the barn kindly inquire as to the success of the ride. My answer to them is always, "it was uneventful therefore it was quite pleasant." I don't know about you, but my definition of an enjoyable trail ride is one that is relaxing, void of drama, while bringing everyone back in good shape without any close calls or near misses. Am I asking for too much? No doubt things out on the trail will happen, but you will be far more prepared for what might come, and will be able to avoid careless mistakes, if you adhere to the 10 rules I've listed below.

1. Never go out alone! It's just not smart! Out on the trail there are many variables. You don't have the control out there that you have over things in the arena.

2. Always wear a helmet! I can't believe how often people think just because they're out on a casual trail ride that they don't need a helmet. I had a dear friend go out with her adult daughter on well trained, well seasoned trail horses. They were both proficient riders and thought it unnecessary to wear helmets. The daughter's horse slipped, which sent them both crashing to the ground crushing her daughter's head onto some concrete and putting her into a coma for quite some time. She survived after months of agonizing therapy but her experience could have been very different had she worn a helmet.

3. Take a cell phone. In this day and age this advice is a "no brainer" and if you feel you don't have a need, bring it along in case someone else does. You could end up being their hero and that's always a nice thing to be.

4. Find your order and keep it. Horses have a pecking order and if you can ride with horses you know well enough it doesn't take long before you know who's happiest leading and who'd rather follow. Don't rock the boat! You can work long and hard trying to change that, but why not accept things the way they are? What do you have to prove, after all... this trail ride stuff is supposed to be for enjoyment. Don't turn it into a stressful battle that can seldom be won in one session, if ever.

5. Never let your horse run back to the barn or up hills for that matter. Horses are creatures of habit and it's far too easy for them to be programmed to take off, especially toward something they want. Think ahead before giving into this common mistake, because someday you won't want to run at top speed as soon as you turn a certain corner and then you'll have NO control. If you must gallop, save it all for heading in a direction away from the barn. You'll thank me for this advice someday.

6. Communicate. Always inform others of your intentions. There's nothing worse than someone "rocking the boat" without warning, tearing off into a blistering gallop leaving everyone behind in a thither. You can get someone severely injured by being so thoughtless and it's never fun or funny to see others lose control of their horse.

7. Know your horse. Is your horse spooky? Is he prone to bolt? Does he cross water? Does he insist on leading? Does he get anxious and jig? If you know your horse, you are better able to be proactive regarding these and other trail issues. Some things you just can't avoid but if you're prepared, you can better deal with challenging situations.

8. Try not to hold too much. Remember, horses get anxious if they're held too tightly by the reins. For a horse to relax, he needs to put his head down and stretch out his stride. This is hard for him to do if you hold on too tightly, both with the reins and with your legs. It can sometimes be a catch 22, but there are ways to override his reactive instincts.

9. Watch your space. Be cautious getting too close to the horses around you. All it takes is one mare in season to give your gelding a good swift kick, because he got too close setting off a predictable chain reaction with the others in the group. Before you know it, there'll be hooves and dust flying with strong possibilities of both horses and riders getting hurt all because someone wasn't paying attention and respecting another horse's space.

10. Never put your horse's hoofs where you can't see! Meaning, never ride your horse in tall grass or anywhere that you can't see through to the ground, if it can be helped. Always stay on a well marked trail! I promise if you break this rule it won't be long before you regret doing so. I thought of this the other day as I was riding along the trail on a client's Palomino when right in front of us I spotted a nice little rattlesnake. Luckily, I was on a well distinguished trail with lots of visibility and had plenty of room to stop and allow the lovely little creature to hurry on its way, but it made me think how if I had been riding through grass I would have never seen it. The same is true for bottles, sharp metal and any kind of trail hazard. Be vigilant in knowing what's below your horse's feet.

These are just a few rules, not all of them but enough to give you the idea that you want to be mindful of the things you do with horses if not for your safety and well being at least for that of your horse. Horses get very upset when their rider falls or is distressed in any way. If you care about your horse, and his sensitivity to you, then you will consider some of the things listed above. Happy trail riding and stay safe!

WHY DRESSAGE?

Dressage is the basis of all proper riding. Founded on balance and relaxation, Dressage sets the tone not only for the horse and rider's training progress, but for their mental development as well. Dressage teaches the rider to connect to their horse like no other discipline and once its concepts are understood, can catapult a rider to newer awareness and proficiency no matter what discipline they choose, whether it be jumping, endurance or barrel racing.

But you're thinking Dressage is hard and it's too technical. If you come away from a session with a Dressage instructor thinking that then that's the wrong instructor for you, because Dressage training should be the most natural and exciting thing you learn from your horse's back. Your instructor should be able to explain the concepts well enough that it makes perfect sense, giving you the ability to gradually implement steps to promote greater balance for both you and your horse.

Dressage need not be hard! I have taught very small children balancing techniques and have had many compete while still quite young, with some on their ponies, walking away with a Dressage show's hi-point score for the day! I tell my adults that come to me with fear of the sport that it's easy enough for a child to do but they don't believe me until they have a child explain the use of the half halt and the importance of the outside rein.

I'll never forget the day I decided my nine year old daughter, in anticipation of her first Dressage show, was ready for a child size Dressage saddle. You should have seen the look on the face of the owner of the largest tack store at the time in Los Angeles when I asked to see their children's Dressage saddles. The entire staff tried to laugh me out of the store. That was twenty five years ago. That store has been closed for some time and no one is laughing now. Today, you can go to any Dressage show big or small and find a good many competitors that are juniors well before their teens.

Let me assure you, learning Dressage will give you a better position and more security in any kind of saddle for any style of riding and better balance and cooperation from your horse in any endeavor. If you think you're doing everything you can to be the best at what you're learning with your horse and you're not learning Dressage, then you've fallen short and will never be the best rider you can be. It is that important.

So, what are you waiting for? Start thinking about looking around at who's out there that could help. Some of the best places to find a good Dressage instructor are at the shows. Look at who's sitting the best, has the calmest horses and seems to be having the most fun with the least amount of stress. Listen to the instructor at the warm up ring. Does her voice sound pleasant with great interest or is she screaming at her rider to "RELAX?!"

You can laugh but I've actually heard instructors do that, scream at a student telling them to "relax." It's rather ridiculous don't you think?

Be cautious looking for the right instructor. Look for someone that genuinely cares about you and not their own ego. If they only want to talk about how great they are, what medals they've won, where they want to go with their own career... run! They are only in it for their own interests. The first question a trainer should ask is for you to tell them about your horse, your desires and who you want to be as a team.

Finding the right trainer can take some time. Don't hesitate to keep looking if you don't find someone that clicks for you. Learning Dressage, as with anything, is best taught by someone you enjoy being with; someone that can make it fun and interesting and someone you feel you trust. If you can find the right instructor I can guarantee you will not regret the time, money and energy spent in the pursuit of better riding skills and greater awareness of the magnificent creature underneath you!

IT'S ALL ABOUT THE OUTSIDE REIN

When I die that's what my headstone will say or at least that's what I jokingly tell my students, because without having your horse in your outside rein you will have no balance, no proper impulsion, no steering, no control and no connection. It's that important!

Look, if your horse is not in your outside rein then it's on your inside rein leading and leaning on the inside shoulder causing it to become unbalanced and almost always resistant to anything else you'd like it to do. Your horse's head will be up, attention focused on everything but you and you will have no control.

Most of the time when a horse acts up it is usually due to improper balance and can almost always be traced to the horse leaning on the inside rein. Episodes of spooking, bolting, tripping and bucking are examples of the kind of resistance you'll experience if your horse is not balanced properly between your seat, leg and hand.

Many times I've been ring side at a show and as a rider on course pulls the horse's head to the outside throwing it onto the inside rein when taking a turn off of a jump I'll predict a buck or bolt and I'm seldom disappointed. Has this ever happened to you?

Show me a horse that spooks at every little thing and I'll show you a horse leaning on the inside rein. It's simply a package deal... improper balance = behavioral problems. I think it's some kind of an unspoken law of the Universe and if you're experiencing such issues you might want to consider your riding technique.

It doesn't matter whether you ride Western Pleasure, Hunters or Reining, having your horse on the outside rein is crucial, but is usually only taught with Dressage training. I'm not sure why this is because it's needed in all disciplines, but it is rare if a trainer that does something other than Dressage knows how to teach the concept. There are so many horses out there going around so unbalanced and it's really a shame because often the horse is reprimanded or worse, labeled as a trouble maker.

Actually when I think of anytime I've been called in to evaluate a problem horse it is ALWAYS because of how it's been ridden with little regard to its balance. And it's seldom an easy fix, because usually there are things I must first teach the horse, such as how to go forward and move away from my leg pressure, but it doesn't take too long, sometimes within one session, but the principles have to be practiced on a regular basis to become the horse's natural way of going.

Of course there are other components involved with teaching a horse to balance, such as the rider's timing in their use of their aids and establishing a steady tempo with the horse's gait. I could take hours trying to explain the

93

techniques, but it would serve no purpose for you unless you work with a trainer and have them demonstrate it. You want to understand the concept and be able to see it clearly or you will only become frustrated.

So what are you to do? Find a good Dressage trainer! Not one that spends all their time boasting of what they know. You must find someone that actually seems to care about YOU! When you find them tell them you want to learn how to keep your horse balanced onto the outside rein to achieve proper balance in your particular discipline. If they can't evaluate and map out a productive program for you and your horse then keep looking.

A good trainer will want to help you to continue along your desired discipline rather than convince you that only a career in Dressage will do. If they try to sell you a line, it's only because they're more concerned with the money and not what they can do to help you realize your own dreams.

So you go to a fortune teller and she pulls out her crystal ball and sees a future for you with a horse that moves steadily, is relaxed and tuned into your every request. She sees a horse that's moving effortlessly with fluidity; one who's confirmation has changed to having a stronger back, stepping farther underneath itself allowing for a lower head and level top line, and she sees you having found the instruction you need to efficiently ride your horse, keeping it balanced and on the outside rein. You can have that with your horse! Proper balance will improve any horse in any discipline! Like I said, "IT'S ALL ABOUT THE OUTSIDE REIN!"

WHEN IS MY HORSE READY TO START JUMPING?

The good news is your horse doesn't have to be perfectly trained to start the process of learning to jump. In fact, starting over ground poles leading to small jumps can keep your horse happier and engaged mentally leading to greater focus and attention on whatever discipline you'd have him do.

Teaching a horse to jump is not just for the Hunter ring. I even knew a race horse owner from Australia that jumped all of his race horses because he felt it helped them to learn to use their hindquarters more efficiently and it's very typical to use cavelletis for Dressage horses for the same reasons. So even though jumping can be introduced early on in your horse's formal training, there are some guidelines you should consider:

1. Assess your riding ability. Working over poles and then jumps requires balance. You must be an effective enough rider to influence your horse's balance while sustaining your own. Anything less would be unfair to your horse. You also will want to have plenty of experience riding in a "forward" position. (If you are unaware of what that means, then you might want to obtain some training for yourself by someone qualified to teach "Huntseat Equitation.")

2. Start small but keep it interesting. You don't want to scare your horse but you do want to give him the opportunity to think. Rather than asking your horse for a big effort, try challenging his mind. He will enjoy the process of learning to figure things out. For this reason I like using what I call "scatter" poles. It's a group of poles strategically placed to look like they were thrown out at random. Allow your horse plenty of rein to drop his head, looking as he steps through the poles causing him to stretch his back and work from his haunches. This is an excellent exercise for a nervous "high" headed horse as it causes them to pause and think before they step and they really seem to like it.

3. Always start with trotting small cross rails. You have far more control at the trot and it's actually more work for both you and your horse teaching you both to improve your sense of timing and feel for one another. Have your horse jumping comfortably from the trot over at least a 2ft vertical before you go on to the canter, starting once again with the cross rails, only this time they can be a bit bigger.

4. Keep the course simple. Even when jumping a course take it one jump at a time. If the horse is not in balance or in proper control it's not the end of the world to circle or pass until you have the horse, or yourself, more together. Don't stress if it's not perfect, just keep in mind the "big" picture and what the jumping is leading to. It doesn't do you, or your horse, any good if you get over the jump only to be racing off at top speed risking your balance, or that of your horse, which can often lead to a tendon injury. It's just not worth it! Remember, be easy with this. You don't have to go to the Olympics tomorrow.

5. Above all, keep it fun! I once knew a brilliant Hunter trainer whose motto was, "if it's not fun then don't do it!" I think this could apply to anything you do with your horse. If you're not happy and having fun with the work then your horse certainly won't be as willing to work hard for you. Think of this in your own daily life, "who are you willing to do the most for, someone who is demanding, unfair, (at least in your mind), unwilling to bend, non-appreciative or someone who's encouraging, gracious, kind and genuinely interested in working with you to accomplish a task?"

By keeping it simple, taking it slow and making it fun you can enlighten your horse's training experience, increase his balance, challenge his mind and build his confidence not to mention enabling yourself to receive a good deal of satisfaction knowing you are responsible for bringing all of this "equine" well being into his life.

HOW IMPORTANT IS MY JUMPING POSITION?

It is everything! If you are to stay in proper balance and control over a jump and influence your horse to maintain his balance while in the air, your position has to be exemplary. I can just look at a picture of a horse in the process of going over a jump and know what the rider's position looks like by the way the horse is using his body. If a horse drops his knees, picks them up too early or jumps with his chest before his knees it's because the rider's weight is balanced upon his neck with seat in the air too forward out of the saddle. This is caused by the rider's leg slipping back behind the rider's seat and not supporting their weight forcing their upper body to do the task balancing on their arms supported by the horse's neck.

If the horse, when going over the jump, drops his back end or drops a pole from behind, it's because the rider has dropped their seat too soon onto the back of the horse. Such a problem exists because the rider's leg is too far forward and cannot maintain its position directly under the rider's seat to support it while out of the saddle.

Often a rider does both with leg too far back and upper body too far forward on takeoff only to lose their leg too far forward on landing throwing their seat back to the saddle causing the horse to not only have difficulty with picking up its front legs on takeoff, but then dropping the back and coming down too soon from behind when landing. This happens when a rider's leg is simply too weak to be in control of where it needs to be kept throughout the ride.

If you ride a horse that is new to jumping and you exhibit an improperly balanced position over and over again, your horse will begin to set up a habit of jumping not only in a way that's not efficient and looks unsightly, but he could potentially hurt himself or you in the process, not to mention the wear and tear on his body over time producing a vast array of soundness issues.

If you ride a seasoned veteran that has been trained properly, and you have an insecure position, you will get a bad fence from time to time, but long term damage will be limited. That being said, any bad rider position will eventually take its toll depending on how severe the balance problem of the rider is. Most likely the old boy will simply start refusing, sensing the rider's instability.

So how do you know what your position looks like? There are all kinds of ways to feel it, but the easiest way to tell is to get a picture from a side view with you in the process of a jump. If your photographer has a camera that can take several frames from take off to landing, so you can view the entire process of jumping, it's a tremendous benefit. Your goal in viewing these pictures is to simply see your weight into your heal with your leg directly under your seat to balance your body in every frame. Many years ago when we all had VCRs my daughter would spend countless hours analyzing videos frame by frame of herself jumping and to this day she has a better position than anyone I've ever seen.

Of course there are other points of good position that range from keeping your eyes and head up, to having your elbows in and directly under your shoulders to your shoulders back with a nice flat back, but without the proper support of your body by your leg being strong enough to stay directly under your seat, the rest of these points of proper position are hard to achieve.

When I start with a rider, it's all about developing the leg, because without the leg staying under the seat in any regard, staying in balance is almost impossible. How do I teach that? Drills! Drills, drills, drills! Constant exercises that call attention to where a rider's leg is, forcing them to keep it into position to maintain their balance during the drills. Much like you would practice scales on a piano or the letter positions on a keyboard, keeping the leg correct must become instinctive to be effective. It has to be second nature and something you don't have to think about so you may go on to tackle more challenging issues. Without being able to maintain the proper leg position, you have no balance. It isn't possible.

Let me share with you some of the exercises I ask my students to practice. See if your balance is challenged when doing any of these?

1. The "Two Point": The "two point" should be successfully executed at the walk, trot and canter (where it's known as the "half seat"). It's when you raise your seat directly off of the saddle keeping it centered and not shifting it forward. In doing so, drop into your heals, stretch your leg down and close your hip angle letting your arms follow forward over your horse's neck. Now you're in "jumping position." You want your leg strong enough and underneath you correctly to the point that you can maintain this position without touching or leaning upon the horse's neck.

2. "Down, Down Up": This is when the rider repeats in rhythm a constant changing of their diagonal at the posting trot over and over again keeping their seat connected between the two strides. When the rider is down in the saddle, the upper body tall and keeping their leg from pushing forward in front of their girth.

3. "Up, Up, Down": This is just the opposite of the above when the rider, during the posting trot, suspends their body into the air in just one extra stride maintaining a rhythm and doing it over and over again as the horse trots without falling back into the saddle. To do this, a rider has to keep their leg under their body to support them while out of the saddle.

4. Gymnastics: When the rider can maintain their position and has been jumping successfully it's time to test their ability to jump without thinking, that's when I put them through a gymnastic line. I keep the jumps in the beginning to small cross rails and build them gradually through a session starting first with ground poles and moving up to the jumps to eventually having the rider continue through the line in perfect form.

When you can successful master all of the above, have those pictures taken again and you'll see the difference in how both you and your horse execute a jump. Make note of your progress and always work to improve by challenging yourself with more difficult maneuvers such as jumping on a curve or on up and down slopes.

The point is to be careful and have fun while building your skills. Take your time and be patient with both you and your horse. Remember, although there are some, perhaps more talented than others, the thing that's most important to improvement is your desire and choosing a willing partner. Make it fun for him and you'll both end up on top of the world!

WHY DO I NEED TO RIDE DIFFERENT HORSES TO BE A GOOD RIDER?

Because every horse is unique and can teach you different things!

Some people ride the same horse, day in and day out, and they can become quite proficient… on that horse. Put them on a different horse and things can fall apart quickly with the rider feeling like a fish out of water. The harsh truth is… you cannot become what is considered a "good" rider if you can only ride one horse.

Every horse is different from their gaits, because of their confirmation; to their personality, because of their breed. Some horses are more sensitive to your seat, others to your leg and some to your hand. There are horses built uphill with their poll higher in relation to their croup making it harder for you to keep your leg back under your seat and horses that are built downhill with their poll lower than their croup making it harder to keep your leg forward and under your seat. (The point being, to stay in balance you MUST keep your leg under your seat to support your core.)

There are faster horses, horses with more energy and sensitivity that take very few aids and slower horses that are a bit on the lazy side who need more leg to move and often stronger cues from your aids. There are lazy horses with big strides that toss you to and fro if your position isn't strong enough to stay centered and balanced and there are high energy horses with big strides so besides controlling your position you must know how to regulate your horse's speed through your seat. Horses with short strides and high energy present a different problem. A rider must learn how to react quickly, almost instinctually, in order to maintain a connection on such a horse. And there are horses with short strides that are lazy which is the best mount for more of a beginner so that they have plenty of time to think about their balance, steering, position and their aids without feeling like they're covering too much ground in the process.

I think you're starting to get the point, which is… you cannot consider yourself a "good" rider until you have developed the skills to adapt to the various questions each horse will pose. And you certainly cannot be an effective trainer without such skills, unless you restrict your clients to only one particular kind of horse which some trainers do.

Some of the riders I admire most can be found at the larger shows known as "catch" riders. They hire out their services as a rider to compete on another's horse. Often they have never met the horse before and have only a few minutes in the warm-up ring to get familiar with everything necessary to go into the show ring and win. What really dazzles me is that often these expect riders are those in the children's ranks who earn money through this practice to pay for their own show expenses when campaigning their own prospect. Talk about learning from hands on experience. These kids can grow up to be some of the best trainers around and usually have illustrious careers at the higher levels of competitions.

Now if you're riding simply for pleasure with your horse as your best friend and the two of your aren't planning to go to the Olympics you most likely have all that you need, but sometimes riding a different horse can clarify and resolve issues or things you need to improve upon in the same way a different instructor can break through a barrier you've had with a difficult concept.

Riding a horse other than your own from time to time can also serve to convince you that indeed you chose wisely, and it can bring you to appreciate more fully what a wonderful match your horse is. In jest I often threaten a student that has a particularly nice horse to put them upon something a bit more uncomfortable just to make them more fully aware of what a four legged gem they have. After some nervous laughter they graciously decline as they give their mount a loving pat as if to say, "You're the best, I'll never take you for granted." I love it when that happens.

So the choice is yours. If you want to be the best and move up through the ranks of higher competition, it benefits you to ride all of the horses you can but if you love the experience of connecting to that very special equine exclusively then you have your answer, and the term, "good rider" can represent more than just a physical application. It can be a term used to describe your emotional journey into the horse world and one to describe the wellbeing that comes from living an equestrian lifestyle.

USING YOUR VOICE AS A TRAINING AID

For the Dressage community, using your voice in any way has been prohibited in competition and so when in training a rider steers away from using such an aid for fear it will affect their performance once they're in the ring but I've been a long time believer in using vocal cues when working with your horse in the round pen, on the lunge line or even under saddle. Even if you can't use those cues in competition I find it valuable to train with vocal commands and take the time to transition going without them into the show ring. At least your horse had a clearer understanding of what you wanted in the beginning when things can be more confusing to him and if the Dressage ring isn't your goal then you're completely free to use your voice anytime you choose.

I felt quite vindicated just last week when a scientific study came back proving that horses learn better and with less stress when vocal commands (aids) are implemented as part of a comprehensive training regimen. The way I see it is that you would want to use anything and everything at your disposal to make what it is you're asking of your horse more obvious, thus eliminating second guessing on the part of the horse thereby reducing his stress level significantly. In fact if you were to look at my training techniques you would discover it's all geared toward the horse's sense of peace and wellbeing by teaching correct principles and letting them govern themselves. You'd be quite surprised to see how well horses relate to such guidance. Keeping things simple, while re-enforcing what it is you're asking, with as many tools as possible, is a part of that system.

When I think far enough back into my horse career (and believe me that's a long time ago) I suppose I've always used my voice but it became even more crucial when I started teaching, particularly when having students on the lunge line. If I have students that are just getting started I want them free to focus completely on their position without the distractions of trying to control the horse and so I want my horse to be quietly responsive to whatever it is I ask of them through my vocal commands. Is it no wonder that my best lunge line lesson horses are the best trained horses overall?

Pair up your voice with the command from your aids (your body language) and you have some significant tools for getting your horse to do just about anything you wish. Not yet convinced? How about, when you use your voice it creates a picture in your mind of what it is you're asking helping to convey those ideas through your body as you organize your aids to request what it is you want from your horse? So not only does it signal to the horse what is wanted but puts the rider in the proper state of mind as well.

More reasons… as a Dressage instructor I often have the opportunity to read a lower level test in competition for my students. Since the horse (and

102

often the rider) has become familiar with hearing my voice I can use it to calm them both as I read through the test. (I could write an entire chapter on how much can be accomplished by reading a test for a competitor.) So even though the rider isn't allowed to use her voice in the test, the horse still benefits from hours of hearing my voice in training.

Of course using your voice doesn't have to be reserved only for cues (although I suppose the horse would take more notice of them if it was) but I use my voice liberally most often to praise and to calm a horse just like I would working with anyone I loved.

The bottom line is taking into account the entire experience. If your horse is more responsive, if you feel a better connection and if the quality of the ride is better because you've implemented your voice then I think you should consider your voice as a vital part of your training regimen.

SHOWING YOUR HORSE

105

WHY DO I WANT TO SHOW MY HORSE?

There are many reasons to show your horse. For some it involves improving upon their horse's training; helping them to be more comfortable in foreign surroundings and teaching them they can survive, even thrive, while under the stress of a judge and an audience's scrutiny. For others it's an evaluation of their own personal horsemanship skills, as well as their horse's training, giving them both a baseline to which further progress is measured. These are both valid reasons for so much time, effort and expense to be invested in participating in a show but I feel the most important reason for a horse or rider to show is motivation.

Do not underestimate the power of motivation in regards to improving the equestrian experience. Believe me it is everything! If I could compare two students, one who plans on showing and one who thinks it's enough just to want to be a good rider I can bet on which student will excel. In all of my years of training, I have never seen the motivation of wanting to go to a show fail to produce a much more focused and determined student and horse for that matter.

Horses love showing too. It's not uncommon for a horse to be their easy going almost lazy self at home but plug them into a show ring and look out! Boy do they turn it on! I'm convinced horses know what's going on in the show ring. They know they're on display and if you make it fun for them they will love it!

Although I will teach anyone regardless of their desire to show, I encourage the student as soon as they are somewhat competent to show because I know then their progress will continue at a greatly accelerated pace. Planning to show enables you to set goals that are more realistic. All show programs have graduated levels from novice all the way to advanced levels so no one needs to be an expert before considering the opportunity to showcase their talents much like a piano student would at a recital.

Yes, there are other things that can motivate a person to want to become a better rider or their horse to be better trained but there's nothing like having to put yourself and your horse's skills against others that seem to want to do just as well as you to keep you coming out for your lessons and make you want to put time into your horse, it will be time well spent!

THE BENEFITS OF AN ACTIVE SHOW SCHEDULE

As far as I can see there are far more benefits than drawbacks to showing and if your horse is young or green when it comes to going to new places then jumping right into a steady routine of showing is the best thing to get your young horse over his fear of new places and experiences.

In an effort to convince you a busy show schedule is worth the time, energy and money I'll start by listing some very good reasons why you may want to consider such an undertaking.

As long as you make it a pleasurable experience for your horse, the more you go the more he'll become accustom to all the fuss and could even learn to look forward to the trailer ride, the new surroundings, the bustle of people and the thrill of the ring.

There's nothing like an upcoming show to keep you motivated to work on training issues. Showing gives us a "deadline" to get things done and as long as you work to keep the training as stress free as possible you will reach far greater goals and get more accomplished by having a time frame in which to build the skills needed for the show ring.

Showing helps you set a "baseline" that your progress can be measured against. You can have a much better idea of where you are when looking at where you've been in regards to the classes taken at shows. And in Dressage you actually have a scored test complete with judge's comments giving you a clear understanding of what's needed for improvement.

As you improve at the shows your horse's value increases. Although his increased value will never be enough to compensate for your training and show fees invested, it will give you the satisfaction of knowing you have created something of greater value in your horse and enable him (if ever sold) to be worthy of a good "show" home with people that often know more about horses and are willing to take good care of him.

It's a rush to see your improvement and win from time to time. Don't underestimate the thrill of victory. It's what spurs us to greater heights and causes us to feel good about all the time, sweat and tears put into our horse. Don't forget to make a big deal over him when he wins. Believe me, he is aware and can feel quite good about himself if you go about it in the right way.

Showing often keeps you on the cutting edge of what's current within your discipline. It helps you to be more confident knowing what's accepted and what's no longer valid, what's the latest in style and what is so last year.

When you show regularly you get to know people. In time you know everyone and a show can provide quite a fine social network letting you meet other people with similar tastes and values and enlightening you to those of questionable character and horsemanship methodologies.

If you keep it fun it can be a wonderful family experience and something to look forward to for the entire family. Everyone can be involved because there's always plenty to do so a victory for the horse and rider becomes one for the team.

I guess my point is that if you're going to show you'll never get that good at it unless you make a commitment to do it often. Doing well at a show just doesn't happen when it's a "once in a while" thing. The horse never learns to enjoy the trailer ride, he never learns to settle into his temporary stall, the rider never gets over her "show nerves" and you can't expect to get far on your training either because the motivation and incentive has left the equation.

I know showing is expensive but if you want the complete equestrian experience, if you want your horse to be superbly trained, if you want him to stay cool no matter what and have him disciplined enough to be under control without you having to control him, then showing is definitely worth the investment.

HOW MUCH IS TOO MUCH SHOWING?

Take This Quiz To Determine If The Price You're Paying Is Too High!

Just as the show season is moving up to full speed and you recognize your ratings are up there in the race for Hi-Point, are the long weekends and the endless training causing you to revisit your choice of chasing after points? Before you throw the whole plan out to regain what was once known as a life, or you spend another weekend moaning the work and frustration of spending so many hours out of your week, take a moment to browse through our list of questions to re-evaluate the value of your show experience.

1. Do you feel like you have no life outside of the show ring? Are you feeling like you'll never have a weekend free again? Do you wonder what it must be like to sleep past 5am on a Sunday morning? Chances are great you'll never know once you've been bit with the Hi-Point bug when the familiar justification of "just one more show and I'll assure my place at the top" becomes your battle cry.

2. Does your horse lack the enthusiasm that he once had when he saw the trailer roll around the barn? We put our horses through a good deal of stress when going to and through a show, at some point the fun disappears and the horse just shuts down.

3. How much does showing take away from your quality of life? Think of all the family and friends that are left behind. If your friends and family are involved with the show and you enjoy the social interaction then you can void out this bothersome consideration.

4. Are there other things you want to be doing? Closely examine why you're showing and whether it's worth giving up other things that help you to feel fulfilled.

5. Do you plan on establishing your name in the horse industry? If this is what you wish to do vocationally then it's of course part of the package and lifestyle, plus finding out if you can do it 24/7 is quite necessary.

6. Do you have to mortgage the family dog to stay in the running? Are you doing without or perhaps even taking on debt to continue your show schedule? If so, you might want to re-visit the early question on why you're doing this and what difference will show success mean to you.

7. Are old friends turning away or trying to avoid a conversation with you because all you can converse about is horse related topics? I actually had this happen to me and found myself having to work at not talking too much shop around others that didn't share my interest.

There is a solution to all of these concerns and it doesn't involve the discontinuance of showing. Instead it only means that you don't chase the points. I know this is easier said than done. Of course you want to sign up for the year's Hi-Point because how would you feel if you didn't and you scored so well that with a limited number of shows you could have won it regardless? No, the answer is to be disciplined enough to not follow the standings, live your life, go to a select number of shows that work with YOUR schedule and simply let the cards fall where they may.

I used to have a teacher whose favorite saying was, "one hundred years from now will any of it matter?" If you find yourself torn between running for the roses and having a life, you may want to ask yourself this question and may the "horse" be with you in all your endeavors.

YOUR HORSE'S FIRST SHOW

5 Sure Fire Ways To Make It A Success!

Whether your horse is green or has been under saddle for years, his first show and the manner in which he experiences that day, can determine his attitude regarding any event for the rest of his life. Seeing this statement as either a promise or a threat can call an owner to action insuring his horse's best interest is kept foremost in a handler/rider's mind, and the day will prove to be a valuable and positive life lesson. If you think you're ready to take the plunge, then you may want to look over the following suggestions.

    1. Ask yourself, "Have I done my homework?" Although, if a rider waits till their horse is perfect, chances are they'll never get to a show. Nonetheless, you don't want to go into the ring unprepared. Make sure the classes you enter are appropriate for the level to which your horse has been trained. Sounds simple enough, right? Yet almost every show I attend I see someone that is in way over their head and the most alarming are the children put into classes by well meaning trainers or parents that haven't either the expertise or the sense to know not only the physical dangers but the psychological ones as well. If the child has a bad experience it can turn them off to a wonderful lifestyle forever.

    2. Who says you have to compete? If it's the very first time your horse is away from the barn why not plan on just hanging out? Take your horse for what we can call a "dress rehearsal" having him and you completely prepared to enter in the slight chance that he goes like a million bucks in the warm-up ring. (Because of insurance, many shows now must have you entered in at least one class to work on the show grounds, but it's money well spent to give your horse an opportunity to be out and about without the added pressure of getting into a class.)

    3. Give yourself ample time! Again, this sounds like a given, yet so often we cut our schedule far too close for a myriad of reasons, everything from having problems with trailering, to forgetting equipment, to waiting around for others to join us. The list is endless and believe me things will come up!

    4. Try to come in early and stable there at least the night before. Having to secure a stall at the showground is a good deal more work and expense but doing so often proves to be a lifesaver. If this is your horse's first time away anywhere you will want to be sure to be on "standby" for as long as it takes to be certain he's happy and comfortable.

    5. Keep it fun! Horses are living, breathing and easily influenced individuals capable of enjoying themselves just like you and I. If you are stressed, think you have something to prove, are a perfectionist and are nervous, chances are your poor horse will be also. If you want to stress about something, make a commitment to insure your horse has the time of his life, so much so that he'll refuse to go back into the trailer to go home. Seriously, it has been on many occasions that I've witnessed such behavior when a beloved mount has discovered the bliss of basking in the limelight of all the attention, the adoration and the company of new found friends.

Going to a show with your horse can be exciting and rewarding as well as the quickest way to cement valuable training concepts but remember it's not about the ribbons. It's about building your horse's self esteem and his feeling of self worth catapulting you both into broader and memorable experiences. It all starts with the first. If you make it pleasant, fun and relaxing it will lead to a lifetime of success!

HOME AWAY FROM HOME

How To Insure Your Horse Is Safe And Comfortable At The Show.

If you think the show ring is stressful, then you haven't had the opportunity to settle your horse into a strange stall at strange show grounds. Many veteran exhibitors can attest to the fact that how well your horse settles into his weekend abode can make or break your chance at a ribbon, at best but, at worst, can be the reason for a full blown catastrophe. Listed below is a step by step accounting of some procedures that need to be adhered to if you're to give your horse a safe and enjoyable experience at his next show.

Let's start at the beginning assuming you're organized and your departure wasn't too stressful.

Step 1 - The Stall: Before you put your horse into it you must scrutinize every inch of it checking for nails, loose boards, splinters, anything that may pose a threat. Check the ground... are there rocks, nails, glass or anything that can pose a hazard? Remember, if there's even the slightest thing that a horse can get hurt on believe me he will find it. If there's something that isn't appropriate, a tough door to open or close, an electrical wire close by or anything dangerous within your horse's reach, don't hesitate to consult with whomever is in charge and ask for a new stall. You have every right to and they want you to feel secure. Often, they'll work hard to get you what you need.

Step 2 - The Sun: Next, check to see what angle the sun moves at. Will it cause your stall to overheat? During the summer months, it's typical for owners to place fans and even misting systems above their horse's stall to keep them cool. Just as mentioned earlier though be careful to not have any electric cord or nail or string where your horse can get to it.

Step 3 - The Water Bucket: Be sure to secure your horse's water bucket so he cannot turn it over or spill it out and be careful it's hung at just the right height. For an average horse, you should have two buckets, one always with fresh water and one with electrolytes. The water should always be kept full because dehydration is one of the most typical ailments at shows. Besides dehydration, if a horse doesn't drink enough water to process his food he could end up colicking, which will bring a quick end to your weekend and perhaps even to your horse. It's a lot of extra work but you might need to also bring with you your horse's water. Many horses don't like the taste of water elsewhere.

Step 4 - Bedding: Always properly bed your stall. This is not the time to skimp on bedding. Use enough to keep your horse from meeting the ground under his body when lying down and be sure to bank the shavings up along the walls. Most show stalls are a bit cramped and you'll want to bank your bedding far up the sides to prevent your horse from getting cast.

Step 5 - The Feed: Be sure to feed your horse at the show the same kind of hay he would eat at home. If you can, you should even bring your feed from home to keep your horse from eating hay from a different region, which can cause him to colic or have an allergic reaction.

Step 6 - Grazing: It's good to have something in front of him at all times. Horses relax when they chew so consider some kind of "grazing" feed to keep him busy and help him to unwind. Something really tasty like a nice Timothy or Orchard Grass will tempt him to focus more on what's in front of him then the Stallion across the barn aisle.

Step 7 - Treats: Be careful not to feed too many treats. It's great to reward your horse, especially when he's being really good, but be careful not to overdo anything in the way of nutrition at the show. A too rich diet can wreck havoc on a horse's system when they're under stress of new surroundings.

Step 8 - Getting Your Horse Out & About: The horse stalls at shows are usually quite small so be sure to get your horse out as often as possible for a walk especially if he's been in a lot of classes that day. After working so hard he will likely get stiff and sore if he's not allowed to keep moving. Besides it gives you a chance to check in with all your friends down the barn aisle to see how they fared in their classes.

Step 9 - Grooming: Keep your horse well groomed to keep him from getting itchy and to prevent him from rolling. Granted, at some point, your horse will want to lay down and perhaps even roll but the risk of getting cast is ever present so the more you can reduce his chances of rolling the more you can reduce the chance of him getting cast.

Step 10 - Bandaging: You may want to consider keeping your horse's legs bandaged if they stock up from being in a small stall but do not, I repeat, do not bandage your horse's legs unless you are an expert or have access to one that will do it for you, because you can do more damage than good putting a bandage on your horse the wrong way. Putting a bandage on your horse properly is almost an art form and takes a lot of experience to master.

So there you have a basic list of things that are mostly necessary. Properly settling your horse is lot of work and there are a lot of things to be aware of, but it's something that must be done right to avert disaster and enable your horse to compete at his best. If your horse isn't comfortable, I can assure you your show will be an unsuccessful endeavor in one form or another. If you're going to all the expense of showing, the time put into your training and all the sweat equity in general, then you want to be sure you will have your best chance of winning and it starts with the comfort and safety of your horse, your partner and your friend.

THE WARM-UP RING

Horse Show Etiquette Checklist

Some typical council I have for a student when I'm attempting to calm their fears regarding their first show is, "you don't have to worry about the show ring, it's the warm-up ring you'll have to survive!" I always love to see my student's stunned reaction to that pearl of wisdom, delivered by me with a coy smile and a gleam in my eye; evidence of my confidence in knowing I can skillfully and successfully give them a good experience amongst circumstances that can be challenging at best.

What you accomplish in the warm-up ring can make or break your achievements for the day, or even set the tone for an entire weekend. Featured below is a list of ideas you'll want to think over to prevent yourself from going in ill prepared or unaware.

Let's start at the beginning: Are you at the show and tacked up with time to spare? I cannot begin to stress this concept enough. Don't think for a moment your horse is not affected by the stress you're feeling from being late and in a rush. Horses are far more sensitive than people to others emotions and you can only imagine what your stress level is doing to them. Remember, early is on time and on time is late! Make this your motto and see if your horse's behavior at shows doesn't change for the better.

Next, keep in mind that the show warm-up ring is NOT a lesson ring! I know some of this involves your trainer and the schooling they provide you with at the show, but I would hope that your trainer has the wisdom to know that the warm-up ring is no place to tackle new concepts! While there are often breakthroughs made at the show, it is far less traumatic to perfect as much of what is expected while in the comfort of your own facility. The key is to keep the "show experience" as stress free as possible and trying to master something new is not helpful in realizing that objective.

Be selective about where you warm up. While there is a specific ring set aside at most shows designated as the 'warm-up ring,' sometimes you have options of more than one, so be sensible and choose one with the least traffic. Even with a seasoned horse, just as in driving a car, you want a certain amount of space to prevent a collision, not to mention subjecting your horse to the carelessness of other riders, or their attitudes that are causing their horse to be on the verge of a meltdown. Horses are very aware of another horse's anxiety and often they cannot help but react.

Be courteous! You should be well aware of the "laws" of the warm-up ring. When passing on-coming horses, stay to your right, just as though you were driving a car, and you'll prevent a lot of embarrassing moments. Try to pass someone going slower than you, and moving in the same direction as

115

you, on their inside not along the rail! If on the rare occasion you find yourself forced to come up along the rail, when in doubt, call it out! No one will mind if you politely notify the rider that you're passing, between them and the rail, but, just as with cars, passing this way can be somewhat hazardous, as it puts you between the rail and the horse being passed with no way out.

Don't crowd the gate or hog the rail! I still can hardly go to a show without seeing someone being very inconsiderate by hanging out inside the warm-up ring, chatting to others over the rail and joining up with comrades and visiting while blocking the paths of those trying to get their horses ready to go into their class. I try to be nice about asking such people to please go elsewhere for the sake of everyone else attempting to do right by their horses, but I fear in my older age I'm becoming far less subtle because I feel this behavior is so blatantly rude I can hardly believe it's not being done on purpose. Please show some class when in the warm-up ring and respect other's rights to have the space needed to get the job done.

These are just a few things to keep in mind the next time you enter the ring. Remember to keep it simple, be thoughtful of your horse and others, and enjoy the opportunity you have to showcase all of yours and your horse's hard work! Have a splendid show!

MYTHBUSTERS

Horses Smell Fear

When Riding, The Horse Does All The Work

A Beginner Needs A Well Trained Horse

To Be An Effective Rider You Must Have Control Of Your Horse

I Can Fix Any Horse

I Can Control My Horse Better With A Stronger Bit

HORSE'S SMELL FEAR

It is my opinion that horses really couldn't care less about our fear and I have proof. Try riding a wild Mustang for its first time under saddle after it went around the ring in a bucking rage in reaction to the saddle being placed upon its back. Believe me, that's fear and yet as many times as I've felt fear, I've never had a horse react to it. Why, because I'm a great actress? Am I so good I could win an Academy Award? No, the truth is, horses only react to what our body language is telling them. Let's look at this concept more closely by making a study of physiology.

What happens to a rider's body sitting on a horse when they feel fear? They tense up. They pick up, pull or squeeze the reins. They clutch or grip tightly with their legs, often leaning forward. Now, let's look at what a rider does to tell the horse to go? They tense up. They pick up, pull or squeeze the reins. They clutch or grip tightly with their legs often leaning forward. Are you starting to get the picture?

The last thing I'd want to do on a wild Mustang for its first time under saddle is tell it to go and go fast. If I let my fear control my body no doubt that would be the signal he'd get and away we'd go, him dashing across the ring and me most likely on the ground.

Now, using the Mustang again for an example, let me explain how I would ride such a magnificent creature and live to tell about it. Remember my mention of great acting abilities? I think the saying, "fake it 'till you make it" generally applies here. After spending plenty of time with my feet resting in the stirrups, I'd settle my seat in the saddle over and over again with the horse just standing there, and then I'd finally sit; just sit and breathe. I'd keep my legs loose, sometimes not even in the stirrups. I'd concentrate on my legs, arms, hands and well frankly every part of my body staying loose. I'd think relax and pet the horse, stroke his neck, knead it as though it were dough and I'd watch his ears telling me he's ready for more. I'd go onto stroking every part of his body and move around in the saddle as I do so. Whether I'd go on from there is up to the horse. If that is all he wants to accept for the day, then that's fine and I can be sure that the next day he'll let me go further and the next and the next. It's amazing how keeping such an attitude always seems to put me on the fast track when starting a horse and I find myself doing things in training that I would expect to take far longer. In other words, the more I can convince my horse that there's no rush, the faster we seem to progress and all of that's done through my body language.

So next time you're terrified to be on a horse, (providing you have no good reason to be), just remember the horse doesn't really care, he only reacts to what your body's telling him and the signals you give him either deliberately or through default. It's your choice, depending on how strong you are mentally and how well you can control your emotions.

WHEN RIDING,
THE HORSE DOES ALL THE WORK

This idea is obviously something only thought of by those who don't ride. Even when riding Western out on a leisurely trail one will feel the punishment to one's body when they dismount at best, but change that to riding a discipline such as Dressage or Eventing and you can be sure the one doing the riding is just as much of an athlete as the one with the four legs underneath, perhaps more so.

It's not enough to simply direct a horse, but in proper riding, the rider not only controls their own balance throughout a multitude of conditions but often is responsible for influencing and maintaining the balance of a 1,200 lbs animal underneath them. Just being able to have enough control over your legs and keep them balanced directly underneath your seat giving your entire body the support it needs while you float effortlessly above the saddle when jumping takes the strength of a triathlete.

Did you know pound for pound a jockey is the greatest and strongest athlete of them all with greater endurance than a marathon runner and stronger than a weight lifter with more agility than a soccer star or karate expert? You don't have to take my word for it... I would challenge any layman to try and last 30 minutes in a formal Dressage lesson and still be able to walk the next day.

Long ago when most of my students were teenage girls, I had them invite all of their "jock" boyfriends to come out and take a spin on the horses. Seems the girls were getting tired of the boys always complaining about their dedication to the sport and going on about it being no big accomplishment to ride. All I can say is there was a lot of education transpiring that afternoon with the girls laughing hysterically as they watched their boyfriends bouncing and falling everywhere pleading (some to the point of tears) to dismount. Those few brief minutes that afternoon were a rude awakening for the young men and they were never again to complain about the horses taking the girl's time.

I'm sure I've been "preaching to the choir" with this article as everyone reading this is well aware of the physical nature of our sport, but feel free to pass this along to anyone the next time an "unenlightened" person makes that age old statement, "I don't see what the big deal is, it's the horse that's doing all the work." Oh brother!

A BEGINNER NEEDS A WELL TRAINED HORSE

Not necessarily. I find this combination is often a problem in that even if a beginner did understand certain advanced concepts they would hardly have enough control of their own balance to effectively relay information to the horse through their aids and could at best confuse and frustrate the horse, they could even possibly get themselves injured because of a miscommunication.

I feel there's a bit of confusion as to what is meant by a "well trained" horse. A well trained horse is finely tuned to respond to the slightest signal. Put a beginner on that horse, and even on a lunge line, the rider can make a disastrous mistake legging the horse in the wrong way or giving the horse the wrong message with their hands. It's just not a good recipe.

Let's look at that term again and instead of thinking "well trained" horse let's change it to a "well broke" horse. Even though I hate the term "broke" I think the best partner for the beginner rider is a horse that is very comfortable under someone, understands basic cues and is not too sensitive being very forgiving of a rider's mistakes. You want a horse with comfortable gaits, one that understands the cues for walk, trot and canter. You want a horse that doesn't have to have a lot of contact either from the rein, leg or seat and understands vocal commands so the student and horse do not have to suffer until the rider begins to understand and controls their aids.

Now, in a perfect world, the horse you put a beginner on will also be involved with feeling responsibility for the rider's balance and the objective of the lesson. For example, I have a lesson pony that goes easily into her upward and downward transitions so as not to jostle whoever is upon her back. She (as is often the case with older mares) is very careful with the student on her back and literally takes great care in keeping them there. She is also quite accommodating in helping me teach the student whatever the concept is almost as though she's the trainer and I'm just the interpreter, challenging the student just enough to keep them growing through their skills. She's quite remarkable but not unique, for there are many lesson horses out there that are worth their weight in gold. If you have one of them you are aware. If you have a chance to obtain one believe me when I tell you they are priceless and seldom sold but often given away to the honored recipient. Where do I find such a horse? Not in an ad, no matter what people say in it. Such horses are rarely on the open market but inherited through long trusted friends. If you purposely search for such a horse you most likely will not find it. I think the only way to find one is to relax and let the horse come to you because it's like the butterfly of love, if you chase after it, it will constantly elude you.

My only recommendation of how to find a great beginner's horse is to immerse yourself within the equestrian community. Take lessons, lease a horse and get as involved as much as possible with the lifestyle. Only then will you be around enough people, hopefully well meaning, to learn enough to know what it is you seek and the difference in what you'll find, that is out there.

Good luck and be careful! There are far too many people in our industry that can see you and your lack of experience coming for miles and they're looking to make a quick buck off of you or wanting to unload something that is undesirable. Also, don't fall in love with the first pretty face. As a trainer of my daughter's long ago, I used to say this about an ugly pony that she fell in love with, one that would do anything for her, "beauty is as beauty does!" That pony was the most beautiful creature on the planet giving my daughter a wonderful and safe experience. My hope is that you can find such a horse or pony!

.

TO BE AN EFFECTIVE RIDER YOU MUST HAVE CONTROL OF YOUR HORSE

I have to admit I'm sure I'm guilty of using that erroneous statement at least once in my instructional career. The truth is, it's not about having control of your horse. It's about having their attention and having control over your own body and balance so that you may affect your horse's actions.

Let's start with the word "control" in regards to your mount. First of all, you can never control a horse! If you think you can you're on your way toward a huge disappointment, because these creatures that we ride and work around on a daily basis are too large for us to ever control. Let's be logical... if you try to control another person what ends up happening? That's right, you set up resistance and resentment within that person and it's no different with a horse, perhaps even more so, considering the horse's free minded nature bred into him for thousands of years. So let's just throw that whole "control" idea out the window. Now let's look at getting the horse's attention and teaching him to focus. Start with understanding that the horse you're working with really does want to please you, it's just that you two do not speak the same language. To effectively get your horse's attention, which is required for him to understand your requests, you must learn his language rather than expecting him to understand yours.

Understanding your horse's language is about studying and learning horse "herd" behavior and using your body language to implement your messages to him. It's a technique that must be practiced long enough to become second nature to you, (a horse reacts instinctively, and you must learn to do the same in response to his actions). There are many schools of thought on how to accomplish all of this and many "experts" that for a price, are willing to teach you, but I caution you when determining whose method you want to implement... do what makes sense to you! I've watched a few of these gurus of "natural horsemanship" work with horses and haven't been able to figure out what in the world they're asking the horse to do? Then I have to ask myself, if I cannot figure it out no wonder the horse is confused and frustrated! The method you choose to use to communicate with your horse must make sense to you! It must be simple and feel comfortable. Don't believe just anyone that can talk a good story or shows you a horse that seems to respond well to him. Keep in mind that a horse is a creature of habit and if the same technique is employed over and over again in time, the horse will figure it out but it doesn't mean that was the most effective or kindest way to go about training him. My advice is to carefully study different approaches to interacting with horses. There are tons of videos and books out there on the subject. Look at a few different techniques and decide what works for you. Go to a clinic, first only to audit without your horse and make an assessment on whether this method would be valuable for you and your horse friend and only then consider subjecting your horse to the experience. Remember it's just like learning anything new that you care deeply about and involves the future of someone you love. Lead with your heart, follow your gut and be willing to ask questions whenever they arise.

Second, keep in mind the use of the word "control." This word should only be used in reference to YOU and your position, your balance and your expectations for what it is you want your horse to do for you. If you're not in control of your body you have no business asking anything of the horse underneath your unbalanced frame! A person not in balance and control of their weight causes all kinds of miscommunication between them and their horse by imposing every kind of mixed signal to a horse causing him to be frustrated at best. I always tell my beginner riders when I put them on my very well trained lesson horses that it's amazing at how the better rider they become the more willing the horse becomes. After I've had a good laugh, I go on to explain that indeed the horse is perfect and that any mistakes are caused through rider error. This is a law that will always ring true no matter what.

The bottom line is that you must have skills! Don't expect to ride well without proper instruction by someone who can make an accurate assessment of what is needed and can play interpreter for what it is the horse is telling you he needs from you to get the job done. Remember, to control a horse you need only to control yourself which could be a great metaphor for life but that's a whole other article. However the thought does lend itself to illustrate the richness of the entire equestrian experience and what it can do for us in transforming our lives in all situations for the better!

I CAN FIX ANY HORSE

I used to think this but I've learned since that there are some horses (just as in people) that are beyond my help. Not realizing this a few years ago nearly cost me my life!

Something to understand is that every horse and situation is different and that you're not God! You can only do your best using all that you know to do. You cannot let the horse's reaction frustrate you to do anything other than move you to take either another approach or give what you're currently trying more time to take effect and only if you're sure it's the right thing to do. Don't let your ego lull you into a false sense of confidence causing you to ignore the signs of trouble and the precautions you would insist on your student taking if you were a professional instructor. Being a good instructor means taking the same advice that you dole out daily and not thinking you're above your own counsel. Also don't let that little voice of scorn inside chide you into thinking yourself weak in conviction by doing what it takes to insure a successful outcome. If you're unsure how your horse will react to your requests take the time to be sure before proceeding. Put the horse on a lunge line just long enough to get a "read" on where the horse is coming from and to establish your communication from the ground before expecting to do so once seated upon him.

If I had taken this advice that one time years ago I would have saved myself from a huge disaster that my body still bears the scars from today. If I had taken a mere ten minutes to gage where my horse's head was the accident would have never happened, but I was determined to do what I considered a simple task and without any regard for my horse's frame of mind I continued along the course planned for that morning. All I can say is thank God I had the good sense to be wearing a helmet, but that's a whole other subject that I feel just as strongly about. So the next time you think you know everything about dealing with a horse that may be challenged in some way, and that little voice inside tells you to think again, keep these few ideas in mind:

1. Have a plan. Remember to simply have a plan with each and every horse you work with and let that horse dictate what that plan needs to involve. Your plan should include realistic expectations as well as alternative techniques.

2. Be flexible. Each and every horse (like people) needs a different approach. Your objective may be the same and some principles of behavior constant, but horse's are individuals and what works for some may not work for others. In fact, even with a single horse their mood (like with us) can change from one moment to the next so be prepared to change course in mid flight it your instincts tell you to do so.

3. Be proactive instead of reactive. Being reactive is what your horse does in response to your actions. That's what a horse does. So when things are not going quite as you expected stop for a moment and ask yourself what you're transferring to your horse to cause him to react in such a way? Being proactive could be as simple as changing your vibrational tone creating a sense of relaxation in yourself therefore causing it to be present in your horse, as well. And, as all of us know, if your horse is not coming from a place of relaxation there's little you can accomplish.

4. Be patient. Even with as many years as I've been training horses I still have to remind myself that some horses "get it" sooner than others. It all boils down to trust and some horse's just have in their nature a greater capacity to trust another while some acquire it through years of rewarding interactions with people and other horses. Remember to keep in mind that if you're dealing with a horse that's had a troubled past it could take years to develop the trust needed for a complete connection. You have to be willing to give your horse the time to evolve at his own pace.

5. Learn to appreciate your horse as a unique individual. We have a large pony at our ranch that is around twenty six years of age and has been with us since she was three. Believe me, she, at such a ripe old age, is still a handful but never has there been a pony that was so loved and appreciated for her vitality, her zest for life and her attitude of thinking she's better than anyone or anything. She is her own person (or pony as is the case) and we thrill to see her demonstrate to students that a horse/pony only allows someone to ride them and only if they ride correctly. She has become the most valued teacher of proper riding and she is fully aware of her station which is evident by how she carries herself, much to the delight of all that see her.

So the next time you go to work with a horse and think you know that horse better than he knows himself take a step back and let that horse tell you who he is before you put him in that box. Learn to work with him and not against him and you'll be pleasantly surprised at what he can do for you from a place of trust and willingness. Take the time HE needs to understand and respond in the way you expect and never move faster than his ability to comprehend and focus.

Lastly, recognize your horse's role as a teacher. Try to allow into your experience the lessons that your horse is trying to bestow upon your mind, bringing you to a place of greater understanding; not just to what it is that particular horse needs, but making you more tuned into others that may come to you in the future.

I CAN CONTROL MY HORSE BETTER WITH A STRONGER BIT

If you believe this you have a disaster in your future! I can all but guarantee it!

Newsflash, using your hands is a very inefficient way of controlling your horse! Too often when a student doesn't have the skills needed to control the horse through their seat and legs or the horse hasn't had the experience to be trained properly a trainer looking for a quick fix will just slap a stronger bit into the horse's mouth. This common practice is so wrong on so many levels I hardly know where to begin, but I'll make an attempt to work through my contempt on the subject of harsh bits to explain, on some coherent level, the ramifications of such an ill-fated decision.

There was once a popular horse expert that always said, "a bit is only as strong as a rider's hands." Since then studies have shown that there simply are some bits more comfortable in a horse's mouth than others and I feel you first should ask yourself, "how happy is my horse with what's in his mouth?" If a horse stresses about what's in there than how are you going to establish a sense of relaxation within him that is so crucial to proper connection?

That being said, if it was only a matter of the horse standing there with the bit is his mouth it would be one thing, but most often it's a student with bad balance and uneducated hands that are subject to a trainer that makes the erroneous calculation that a stronger bit is in order. I get so frustrated at this ignorance I want to scream because it is the horse that will be damaged!

It's bad enough for a kind and willing horse to put up with a rider bouncing uncontrollably upon their backs, but throw into the equation the punishment that such movements cause to the horse's mouth makes it intolerable for me to think about because the pain the poor horse is suffering is incredible! Now add to that picture that novice riding with a harsh bit in the horse's mouth and you can imagine the horror that the horse goes through. People call this training? Shame on them and shame on you if you're allowing a trainer to dictate what you know in your heart is wrong and you know in your heart has to be a better way. I assure you there is! Although it will most likely take some time to produce, because it will involve work on your part; training your body to be in better balance and your horse to respond to such.

You have a choice to go for the "quick fix" which I guarantee will someday come back to haunt you or take the time and go to the effort to do the right thing and learn how to properly ride and communicate with your horse so there's no need for a strong, harsh bit. In fact, when a horse is properly trained and ridden there's no need for a bit at all. You don't have to take my word for it. There are countless examples of people riding without any bridle in every discipline. Are these people freaks of nature or amazingly talented horse whisperers? No, not at all! They're people willing to take the time to learn how to ride and convey their requests to their horse the RIGHT way! So if your trainer decides you need a stronger bit it might be time to look for a better trainer. Use your inner knowledge to decide. It's never wrong!

KIDS & PONIES

IT'S JUST A PONY RIDE, RIGHT?

Parents, BEWARE! Don't underestimate the power of the PONY!

But you don't have to take my word for it. If you need further evidence of the dangers of letting your child get bitten by the pony bug you need only consult that great resource of social documentary; you guessed it, none other than "The Simpsons." If you haven't seen the episode where Lisa falls hopelessly in love with a pony and her Dad, "Homer", works and worries himself to exhaustion bringing it all to a sad ending where Lisa has to give up her beloved bringing tears even to the stoic riding instructor's eyes, then I recommend you rush over to your favorite search engine to see what lies in your future. If you have seen the episode, then you must ask yourself, "what the devil were you thinking letting your kid sit upon that pony?" Hey, this is no laughing matter. I'm not trying to be funny, this is serious! Good pony experiences are like potato chips, you can't stop at one and they're frightfully expensive and more addictive than drugs. First time users are often hooked for life, but before I scare you completely away from even entertaining the possibility of this happening to your child, let me describe what can be gleaned from a positive interaction between a pony and your little darling.

First I must admit, horses and ponies teach us so many things that they're worth every dime invested. They are more in touch with their "inner being" meaning they are true to themselves and ask little of us. Your child can learn to love unconditionally, seeing themselves through the eyes of their pony. Your child will learn that respect is a two way street and that integrity is about morals in how you treat someone or something.

Trust can be a big issue both for the pony and the rider, but the right instructor can orchestrate a magnificent union between the two creating a bond that can last a life time, at least in memory. A good instructor can also mix lessons in both instant and delayed gratification, as skills are mastered and self confidence established; life lessons the student can take with them far into the adult world.

Both growing girls and boys flow more easily through the awkward teen years if they've spent some time learning to control their balance atop a moving steed. Grace and elegance are some of the physical attributes proficient riders possess not to mention the body language of confidence they obtain by simply being comfortable around such a large animal.

Listed above are qualities that are almost tangible, but what I have yet to mention is simply the entertainment value, the thrilling exhilaration sitting on top of a moving, almost flying, animal racing across hills or over jumps, jumping into the water, showing discipline in competition or just strolling down an enjoyable trail with friends. Winston Churchill once said, "The back of a horse is good for the inside of a man." No truer words were ever spoken.

What would giving all of this to your child be worth? How can you put a price on an experience so magnificent, so rewarding and so beneficial to your child's future development? The right equestrian experience could make your child's entire future but I must warn you, it has to be the "right" experience. You must diligently seek out an equestrian instructor that not only knows the horse and successful techniques to accomplish realistic goals but also brings a sense of fun and camaraderie to the stables so your child learns a sense of community, allowing them to develop the social skills necessary in life. Finding the right trainer can be a daunting task, but one well worth the time and effort. So what are you waiting for? Be diligent, but be careful choosing. Frequent the shows and look for the barn that's having the most fun while getting the most accomplished in the show ring. Watch at the warm up ring for the trainer that's on top of things, in a calm but energetic manner, and speaks positively about what needs to be accomplished. Search out the trainer that walks the fine line of empowering their students to ride with confidence without being reckless and who recognizes if anything does go wrong it's almost always due to a rider's error; the horse should never be blamed. Look for the trainer that treats their horses, and those of their students, with kindness and respect for the magnificent beings they are. How a trainer treats their horses will tell you how that trainer will ultimately treat your child and their equestrian experience with them.

When you find that trainer, book that introductory lesson. Give your child the gift that keeps on giving. (And taking from your wallet, sorry but had to be fair about this). The truth is, in all the years of raising my daughter with the horses, and with the fortune I spent on the endeavor, I do not regret a single dollar. If I had to do it all over again, I wouldn't change a thing. Isn't that a wonderful thing to be said about something? No regrets! Ah, consider the possibilities!

FINDING YOUR CHILD'S FIRST HORSE

My sympathies go out to any parent searching for their child's first horse. It's a daunting task because there's so much at stake. The right horse can set the stage for a childhood of discovery and lessons in love, patience and goal setting, while establishing a belief in one's self. The wrong horse can create turmoil that can scar your child for the rest of their life. Sound like fun?

With the risks so high, what compels a parent to take the plunge? Well, for me, it was the heartbreak of always finding my daughter's favorite pony or saddle at the stable already booked regardless of promised reservations, relegating her experience to something less than what we had hoped for. (It's heartbreaking to see your child pine away over a pony as it walks by with some other child on its back.)

When you begin to shop for that perfect animal you often suffer from delusions of grandeur. You think that you want the most magnificent, fire breathing steed that will take your child all the way to the Olympics. For me, it was ponies. What I wanted for my daughter was the flashiest, fanciest, most talented pony alive. The problem was they were usually the ones with the biggest balance issues - therefore behavioral issues. When a pony is highly trained, and highly tuned, the last thing they need on their back is some kid that isn't and so we went from one pony to the next and that was both dangerous and frustrating for my child. It took me two ponies, that we had owned, and one that ended in heartbreak through a lease that brought me to understand my daughter simply needed a best friend that she could trust in and one that was trained perfectly for her stage of riding allowing her to just have fun.

What we ended up with people would surely consider a step down in quality from the others we had owned. His name was "Cookie Monster" and he was a frumpy little pinto pony, tons of hair with a spritely little trot, lovely canter and a heart of gold. He would jump anything from any angle, canter readily, but softly, and take my daughter safely off onto the trails for hours on end.

One Christmas vacation when my daughter came down with the flu, the entire two weeks off from school, I brought that little pony right into the house and up to her bedside. She was overwhelmed with joy at getting to love on her pony right there in her bedroom. That became a defining moment in my daughter's childhood and I had that little pony to thank.

Cookie Monster set a path for us leading towards one great horse after another. Had it not been for him, not only would my daughter's horse experience been quite different, (if at all), but I feel I can say in all honesty he changed the course of my daughter's entire life leading her to one success after another.

I cannot stress enough how important the right horse or pony will be, not only for your child's equestrian experience but for their life in general! The quest of finding your child's first horse is not something to take lightly and yet you must know that you can't become too anxious or else you most likely will end up with the wrong horse. You need to walk a fine line between being proactive in the search and staying casual enough to expect that perfect situation to come to you. Here are a few steps to keep in mind when looking:

Have a trainer you trust. Someone whose bottom line isn't how much of a commission they'll make on the sale. A good way to tell is to look around the stable and see how many of his/her clients still own the same horse after a number of years. If the horses in the barn come and go pretty regularly you might want to consider going elsewhere.

Tell everyone, especially those you trust you're looking. Vets, farriers and feed store workers that know you are all good places to start. Talk to those who you've shown with and others in your child's chosen discipline. For example a good Western Pleasure horse will certainly be quite different from that of a Gymkhana.

Get an education. Not just for your child but for YOU! Don't put your child's future at the mercy of a trainer that may not really know you or your child. Do our homework and know some things about what you may or may not want in a horse for your child. Would you know if a horse trots sound? Do you know what makes good confirmation? Do you know what it means when the Vet tells you they see navicular changes in your potential horse's x-rays? You need to know what you're getting your child into.

Get enough training under your child's belt so they can make an educated choice. This is a tough one if you have less than an ideal situation. After all, it was the lack of control of my daughter's original riding experience which caused me to take the drastic step of ownership. The ideal scenario is to have a fun, social barn for your child to train in with lots of different ponies or horses to choose from. Try to rotate them regularly so your child doesn't get stuck on a favorite, which can lead to a great deal of discomfort.

Steer away from newspaper ads. Although there are exceptions, I always tell people that horses and ponies are listed for sale for a reason. Meaning, if it's a horse worth having then it most likely would already have someone waiting to buy it. The best horses never make it into the want ads and after all… isn't that what you're looking for?

Let your child decide. Never stick your child with something they aren't completely thrilled with. I'm a big believer in chemistry. I have seen horse/child combos that had no business happening, (my daughter's first horse for one), and looking back I marvel to think how really perfect it all became because of her commitment. Truth is there will always come a day when it's only the chemistry that keeps things working. If your child falls in love with a certain horse there may be a very good reason. Pay close attention, believe in them and do what it takes to make it happen.

Lastly, remember not to get ahead of your child. If they're in a good program with many ponies to choose from and you're both happy with the experience then hold out for as long as you can before you start looking to own. The more training your child and you can get under your belt, the easier it'll be to know what horse is best. Keep things light and fun, stressing at all times the benefit of riding many different horses, (every horse teaches us something different).

When the time comes where ownership becomes the ideal option, let it come to you. Stay busy learning and look at it all as some grand adventure. Keep yourself in a good place so when that horse does appear you'll know it. When you've made a decision remember that your power of appreciation will cause that horse/pony to be just what you had imagined.

HOW YOUNG IS TOO YOUNG FOR MY CHILD TO START RIDING LESSONS?

Five Questions A Parent Should Ask Before Booking That First Lesson!

With the love of horses striking some children at an early age, a parent often asks how soon they should get started with their child's equestrian education. I've listed below some ideas to consider that may help you decide when it's right for you and your child to start.

1. How great is their desire? Although it's advantageous to a parent's budget to hold off for as long as possible when giving their child formal training in riding horses, some children just can't wait. I have seen children from as young as age three completely obsessed with being around horses and there is an advantage to starting them very young before the world has convinced them large animals are something to fear.

2. How important is it to you for your child to ride? Horseback riding lessons are not only expensive but very time consuming. I suggest a parent doesn't consider lessons unless they can commit to the child's training becoming part of their typical routine. It just isn't fair for a parent to get a kid that loves horses started only to decide their budget of time or money can't accommodate the expense.

3. What are your expectations? Let's be reasonable, obviously a three year old will not progress as quickly as a seven year old, but I have to admit there are exceptions. Of course the earlier a child is started, the farther along they will be at a younger age and the more natural riding a horse will become. (There are medical studies involving the effects of motion to the development of the inner ear in young children and the benefits to a child's overall development.)

4. Can you find a Trainer? Many riding schools will not take a child under the age of seven and for good reason. If the school involves group lessons then the personal supervision needed for a younger child to stay safe is not available. You will have to look long and hard to find a suitable trainer for a much younger child. Such trainers are few and far between, but they are out there. To find one I suggest you frequent some local shows and watch for who's in charge of the youngest riders. You will also want to assess their personality and rapport with the children and whether or not they foster confidence in the rider through positive re-enforcement.

5. Consider abbreviated instruction. Some trainers will allow a young sibling to tag onto the end of a family member's lesson. Even a supervised walk around to cool out the horse can be enough of a positive experience to foster confidence; the ability to move with the horse prepares the child for what's to come into their future.

The bottom line is, if you're willing to give your child whatever time is required, let them move at a speed that is suitable for their development. Find a qualified and cautious instructor with trustworthy equine partners and be willing to pay for their valuable time and expertise. If your child has a strong desire at such an early age to have an equine experience, then by all means find the opportunity to foster that love of horses in them. I can promise you no regrets and only the satisfaction, you as a parent will discover, from giving your child something that can affect them positively for the rest of their lives!

GOOD THINGS COME IN SMALL PACKAGES

Five Reasons For Looking At A Compact Model.

Ok, I have to admit I'm bias, but indulge me with a few moments of your time while I plead the case for starting your child's equestrian career on a pony, as opposed to a horse. I understand circumstances can dictate otherwise, but if you have the option there are many advantages to having your little one learn how to ride on something more his or her size.

1. Size ratio. It's just healthier for a small child to work with something more to their scale. The child often feels greater comfort and more confidence in dealing with something at their level.

2. Grooming and ground work. Obviously your child can obtain greater awareness of his mount when it's small enough for him to do his own grooming and tacking up, giving the child rider a sense of satisfaction and accomplishment along with empowering him to feel a stronger connection.

3. Learning to ride more instinctively. Because ponies are small they move quicker often giving the child no time to think about their balance. This can be a disadvantage if not utilized in the proper way. With the right instruction, a child can learn to balance without having to think about it. Mastering the skill of proper balance will continue to serve them throughout their equestrian career enabling them to be a greater rider for a longer period of time.

4. Dealing with difficulties. I will agree that even the well trained pony can often challenge their rider. There's just something in them that makes them a bit difficult from time to time. How great for a student to learn to deal with resistance on something that can be safer because of its size.

5. Forming a connection. It's easier for a young person to learn unconditional love and bonding with something that they can be solely responsible for. It's a wonderful thing for a child to feel the satisfaction of knowing that they can handle and care for their pony all by themselves. It fosters in that child a desire to do more for their charge, spend more time with it and being responsible for something important. Such confidence has a way of spilling over into a child's experience with other responsibilities such as school, other interests and family.

Size can definitely make a profound difference in your child's equestrian experience, one that can possibly shape his or her entire future at the barn, as well as out in the world. So next time you have a choice in what size equine your child rides, don't rule out the opportunity to realize the many benefits of keeping things small. It is said that 9 out of 10 Olympic riders started out on ponies! Have your child get the most out of their equestrian experience; consider starting them on a pony!

FEAR OF FALLING

Falling off of your pony is scary! If the fear of falling keeps you from enjoying your pony then keep reading for some ideas on how to avoid that sinking feeling that comes from being afraid.

1. Know why you fell off of your pony! Don't even think of getting back on until you and your trainer can figure out why you fell off in the first place! This is the most important step of all! It's not about being tough and just getting back up there, because if you do you most likely will simply fall again and instill a fear in your pony, (ponies don't like it when you fall off), or end up creating a habit of fear in your pony.

2. Stay out of the "danger zone! Was it something your pony spooked at? If so, stay away from that place long enough to build your pony's and your courage and take the time to settle your nerves, as well as your pony's, before you return.

3. Secure your position. Although your pony can give you a really good jolt when he abruptly changes his direction or speed you CAN school yourself to have such a strong and secure position that you won't come off of him no matter what he does. I have seen it for myself when my student's pony stopped so hard he plowed through a jump but my rider never once moved her position in the saddle. There are many exercises your trainer can put you through that will teach you to react through your position instantly and instinctively while staying tight on your pony.

4. Don't try to do something you're not ready for! This is usually the biggest cause of falls. Your trainer needs to be very aware of what you and your pony are capable of and NEVER let you or God forbid, ask you to cross over your limit just to see if you can survive. If your trainer does this to you then RUN as fast as you can to a new trainer; hopefully one that will stay with the basics long enough to insure your success!

5. Fear is your friend! Let it help you to recognize when to take a step back and revisit the successful lessons of the past or perhaps find more training or schooling for your pony from another more accomplished rider.

My point is that falls don't have to happen but when they do, rather than being scared, try to learn from what has happened. If you don't learn something about your pony or yourself during the experience then it has been a fall that has been wasted. If you do learn something from your fall, then you'll look back and be grateful for it happening and be able to laugh about it and move forward with confidence through your riding experience.

DOES MY PONY NEED TREATS?

If you're asking should you look for every opportunity to praise your pony or tell him you think he's special or he deserves a reward then "YES." Ponies are just like every other animal or even people for that matter, in that they know when they're being praised and when they've done something good. Acknowledging them with a treat after they've performed particularly well not only causes them to feel special, but it gives you a warm feeling knowing you recognize your partner's efforts and it actually helps you to appreciate him more and feel a deeper connection. However, there are guidelines you'll want to observe to keep from turning your little darling into a monster.

Always wait until you're ready to put your pony away before giving him a treat. Ponies have a one track mind and if you feed him his treat before you groom him or when you're cleaning him up after his ride he'll hardly be able to stand still and will make life quite miserable for you in the process.

One cookie is plenty, but no more than two. Ponies are very "easy keepers" which means a little goes a very long way. You must always be careful of your pony's weight to insure he doesn't end up foundering. Too many cookies can put him on a very painful fast track to a horrible condition called founder. Carrots are a bit safer but you still need to be careful limiting his reward to only a few.

If you're feeding carrots for treats break them up into small bites and feed them slowly. Ponies are notorious for gulping their food and it's possible for a large piece of carrot to become lodged within the pony's throat and can cause him to choke which can be a very dangerous condition. We once had a pony at our barn that began to choke on pelleted feed causing us to call out the vet and spend a very anxious hour or more trying to save his life.

Be careful feeding your pony from your hand. Since ponies have a hard time being able to tell where the treat ends and your finger begins NEVER reprimand your pony for accidently biting a finger, as they just can't tell the difference. If you want to be smart and safe, put his cookie or carrots in a small bucket and feed them to him while you hold it, that way he can be sure they're from you.

Don't let your pony hold you hostage. Because of their size, I have found this to be more of a "horse" problem than a pony problem in that the horse may become aggressive regarding a treat. When this occurs you must stop feeding the horse treats immediately, relying only on verbal praise and a good pet on the neck for future praise.

Remember to keep in mind that feeding your pony a treat is as much for you (maybe more) then it is for him. Don't let him take advantage of your generosity and in the case of treats, less is always better than more. More love does not mean more treats!

IS YOUR PONY EATING YOU OUT OF HOUSE AND HOME?

Ponies love to eat! In fact, it's the number one thing on their list of what they love to do, much like it is with a horse but with a pony it can be very dangerous. Ponies are known as "easy keepers." That term means they can exist on very little food. The reason they're easy keepers goes back hundreds, or perhaps thousands, of years ago with them evolving from larger horses that became stranded due to shipwrecks, etc., on the islands off of Europe such as Wales, Ireland and England. To enable them to survive on the islands with very little food, they grew smaller and smaller over many generations creating the pony we know today. Pound for pound a pony uses less fuel because its body became more efficient at using its nutrition, therefore you must be careful not only in what you feed your pony but how much. Today, it's much easier to have a broad spectrum of hays to choose from with many options more suitable to a pony's needs. Rarely should a pony be fed Alfalfa. It's simply too rich in nutrients and can cause a pony to easily founder (a painful, crippling and sometimes fatal condition).

Grass hays are much better for your pony. In general, Timothy or Orchard grasses being the best but these hays also come with a bigger price tag. Something commonly fed is Bermuda. Its price is much lower than the others, but be very careful because Bermuda has been known to bind up the intestines causing colic and in my opinion should only be fed when other alternatives are not available. Oat or grain hay may be acceptable, but again you must be aware that its protein and carbohydrate content is much higher than the grass, although not as high as Alfalfa. Regardless of what you feed your pony, you still must keep a close eye on his weight to insure he's not being overfed.

Never feed your pony grain! Absolutely under NO circumstances would you feed a pony grain! They simply cannot tolerate it within their system. It's far too rich causing the pony to possibly founder or colic and it just isn't worth the risk!

Founder is a dreaded condition that sets up inflammation within the leg of the pony causing the coffin bone to rotate and like a cork screw, it begins pressing down into the pony's foot and in drastic cases actually pierces the sole of the foot which often proves to be painfully fatal. Keep an eye open to spot founder quickly. Although horses can also develop the condition of founder it is more prevalent in ponies because it's far easier for them to become obese. Be aware of your pony's habits. If he appears to be in good health but is spending too much time lying down, that could mean his feet are hurting and should be addressed as founder being a possibility.

Be careful keeping ponies on grass. Even though grass is a preferred feed, if your pony is kept out in a pasture be very careful in the spring when the new grass comes in far too abundantly and is particularly rich. You may have to keep your pony in his stall limiting his pasture time to keep him from eating too much.

Remember, ponies can eat as much as a horse but need far less food, so you must be diligent in safeguarding what it is your pony eats. The good news is that ponies live to be much older than most horses with fewer health issues, so if you're careful and protect your pony's well being, you'll have him in your life for a very long time!

SHOULD I CARRY A CROP?

Some kids think it's cruel to carry a crop when riding their pony. It isn't about using a crop with your pony; it's about "how" you use it. Here are some guidelines that will assure you stay your pony's best friend:

1. **Never use a crop as punishment.** If you're hitting your pony with your crop out of frustration or anger, your pony will become resentful and resistant meaning he will no longer like you and will not want to work with you.

2. **Do not use a crop instead of your leg**. I've seen too many children hitting their pony with their crop because they were too lazy to squeeze with their leg to get their pony to go forward. You've probably seen it too?

3. **Use your crop to remind your pony you've asked with your leg for him to go forward.** After you've given your pony a clear signal with your leg to move forward using a squeeze or sometimes a bump and your pony doesn't hear you, then tap sharply behind your leg to call attention to what your leg has asked him to do. After you've tapped with your crop repeat the command with your leg and most ponies will happily move forward.

4. **You can use your crop as an extension of your arm.** If you've used your crop properly your pony will actually welcome a pet with it and you can use it then on a shoulder or a rump to calm and assure a nervous pony by stroking him with it as you would your hand.

5. **Practice carrying your crop so when you do need to use it you don't fumble and drop a rein or jerk on your pony's mouth.** For some, it can take quite a bit of practice carrying a crop comfortably. Don't wait until you need it to get used to holding one.

These are just a few suggestions on how to properly use your crop. I'm sure now you have the right idea. It's just like with the use of any horse equipment; you can use it kindly or with cruelty determining whether your pony will be your friend or your enemy.

PARTING THOUGHTS

The Disposable Horse

Weekend Warriors

Barn Angels

The Horse Rules

Horse Care Tips

THE DISPOSABLE HORSE

There may be many people within our thriving horse industry that will be offended when reading this chapter, but this is a subject that needs to be addressed because all over this country in various backyards and unattended corrals sit horses that are ill cared for, and often neglected, because they have been passed around until no one is sure of who they are or what they've existed as. Other horses are lucky, although still within the backyard environment, that they've found a loving home with default owners that are knowledgeable in caring for such a high maintenance pet, but it seems the majority are more like the first talked about, whose caretakers are people of indifference with poor understanding and skills in equine health and well being. Little thought or consideration is afforded these unfortunate horses because they are no longer what was once an animal that was new, exciting to own and usable. Now they've become either no longer "usable", greatly misunderstood, expensive to keep and/or perhaps even something to fear.

The above mentioned is often the scenario for what has become the "disposable" horse; often tossed out with about as much thought and consideration as one would give a sandwich bag after lunch. Such a horse usually starts out in life well bred with impressive heritage, excellent confirmation and plenty of talent. They gradually move up through the ranks as their training becomes more specialized and their accomplishments add up, but at almost any point in a horse's career they can be sold and moved elsewhere. As the years move on, the horse continues to be bought and sold perhaps at first moving up in his life's experience but over time, and after age and injuries set in, he gradually starts the spiral downward to what end, no one can be sure of. Often these horse's lives are relegated to a brief pat on the head (if they're lucky) and the chucking of a flake of hay thrown over a fence. Many are left without any shelter to stand in the pouring rain or the blistering sun at the mercy of biting insects and, there is little to no routine veterinarian or farrier care. What were once well maintained horses, perhaps even loved by someone in their earlier lives, are now relegated to merely disposable and all because someone in their life experience decided to "move on" for an entire list of reasons that range anywhere from needing a more athletic horse for competitions, to wanting something more befitting the standard of the discipline, to not wanting to put the work of training into the horse to make him more suitable for the show ring, because they were made an offer they couldn't refuse or just because…

How did the disposal of a horse become such an accepted practice and mindset? Granted, there are some very acceptable reasons for parting with a horse. One cannot delude themselves that as a beginner they can stay with the same horse all the way to reach their final goals (although there are exceptions). Then there are the children that eventually outgrow their ponies (and one would never want to undermine the value of the child having something more suitable to their size). Then there's the rider who has professional aspirations and needs to part with a horse to afford moving up through the ranks. Other reasons for having to sell a horse could be lack of funds, or a rider outgrowing their mount competitively or age and illness either by the horse or rider but all of those aside, the biggest reason horses are bought and sold is because of the trainers in this business.

Being brutally honest I must tell you there are few incentives whatsoever for your trainer to encourage you to keep your horse, because it is an industry standard for a trainer to charge a 10% to 20% fee every time a horse is bought or sold within their influence. Why should a trainer want to find you a horse you could keep for many years when there's little or no money in it for him? Or, for that matter, why should your trainer look to find you a more reasonably priced horse, or negotiate to obtain you a better deal on the purchase of your horse, when they would be making less money off of the final sale?

Personally, I find there's a huge conflict of interest when a trainer charges their clients for the buying or selling of a horse, and often the trainer works with the seller cutting a deal behind the buyer's back so he's not aware of the payoff! As if that wasn't bad enough, there are even trainers that work it from both ends; charging both seller and buyer for his considerations and approval causing the price of a horse to sky rocket after all the commissions are doled out. Put that together with the fact that if your trainer finds you a horse that he knows will not be suitable it's a "win-win" for him, because six months down the road he can convince you of that fact and you'll have to turn around and do it all over again while he pockets his 20%+ of the proceeds for each transaction. What ends up happening within the equestrian community, because of this, is a constant flow of horses being marketed and it's not exclusive to the bigger show circuits. This common practice has for generations been seen throughout the entire equestrian industry in every discipline from A shows all the way down to the local level when the minute a horse is no longer perfect for whatever the criteria may be, he is quickly listed for sale because there's money to be made primarily for the trainer. Even when a horse is winning, trainers convince their clients that this is the time to sell because the horse's value is at a premium and they can always take their profit from the sale to "re-invest" in a green horse and do it all over again. Would you do this with your beloved family dog? Why is your horse any different?

Since when did it become acceptable to mindlessly disregard such a noble creature and willing partner? In a society where no one can imagine buying a dog or cat with the intention of sending him down the road almost

147

instantly when he no longer looks like what is fashionable or may require training for a certain issue or simply because he's no longer the newest thing, yet we think nothing of doing such things with our horses.

So what is the solution to this aspect of our present day "throw away" society? Before we address that question, I'd like for you to keep in mind one thing... once you let go of your horse, no matter how convinced you are of his future treatment, you give up your ability to have control over where your horse goes. There's nothing more excruciating to a former owner than to have to stand by and watch their beloved friend be neglected, misunderstood or in the extreme situation, even abused. I know the anguish of sleepless nights, because of the worry that in the pouring rain your relinquished pet could be hungry, out in the cold or in pain when you've tried everything to convince the current owner to sell him back to you, only to have them be more determined than ever to own something you desperately want.

I had a client from Australia who was so determined to never suffer through such torment, that she bought a farm up in Oregon just for the intention of keeping all of the horses that would no longer serve her. She settled them in peace and comfort, cared for by someone that she knew she could trust, complete with her own home on the ranch so she could go up and visit with her old friends whenever she could. Of course, most of us don't have the financial security to afford such a luxury, but I admire her because she did give up the money she could have spent on other things to do what her integrity dictated and she never once regretted it. I still get glowing reports from her of the ponies approaching their thirties that I had worked with for her and it causes my heart to soar to know someone has done it right!

Other ways to at least get closer to safeguarding what happens to our horses when we sell them is to have a "first right to refusal" agreement. Take your time to draft this document and have it stipulate that if the horse you're selling is to once more be sold you get the first shot at it. Of course, this does nothing to insure the current owner, or their trainer is treating him right, but it does bring you some comfort.

I'm also a firm believer in trials. Call it a lease, fill out paperwork, require deposits, make the prospective buyer obtain vet insurance or do whatever it takes to create a comfort level for you, but if you really care about where your horse is going you'll want to know he's not only happy in his new surroundings but is a good match to his new owner so he doesn't continue to be passed along. Some sellers will agree to a one week trial and I suggest only after a pre-purchase exam from their vet. But, to really be sure of a horse working out, I feel a good solid month complete with your right to "opt out" at any time during the trial, and your freedom to come and go at any time to check on your horse while at the new owners, is necessary. If you

148

truly believe in your horse and want him to have the best, you'll consider this option. Just be sure to be careful and get everything in writing and ask for whatever security you need to feel good about it all.

More than anything, you need to follow your heart when it comes to parting with your horse. Ask yourself what you're in this for, what's the price to be paid and who's going to benefit the most? Don't hesitate to "call out" your trainer if something doesn't seem right or fair or logical and above all... do what makes you happy! Do what you know is right, not just for you but for your horse! If you don't know who's buying or where he's going or whether or not he'll be happy, then don't do it! There are ways to be sure of such things. Take the time necessary to know, without a doubt, that the people you're selling to will not only appreciate your horse as much as you, but perhaps even love your horse more than you are capable of! Wouldn't that be a wonderful thing?

WEEKEND WARRIORS

You'd like to spend each and every day with your beloved horse but work, family and a multitude of responsibilities combine to make it impossible for you to attend to your horse through the week. If you're lucky and all of the stars line up perfectly, you can whisk yourself away from the soccer games, the shopping and guilt trips long enough to spend some time, only on the weekends, to be with your best friend.

Ok, I get it. You don't have to defend yourself to me. If I didn't do this for a living I would most likely be in the same situation and daily I'm amazed at the sacrifice my clients make to spend time with their horses. Really, I just don't know how they do it and I admire them for making the commitment and sticking to it no matter what. For those who can't squeeze out that time each day, let me offer a few suggestions that might help you make the most of the precious time you do get to spend with your horse.

Board your horse at the right facility. One that understands and can accommodate your needs. Look, it's simple; horses must be out daily and the more time the better. If your horse doesn't live in a pasture or large enclosure then he MUST be turned out each and every day and for more than just a mere 20 minutes. Even if he does have the luxury of dwelling in a large space, he needs some interaction each day just to help him feel secure. I've worked with horses with abandonment issues because they feared the loss of their special person. Your horse needs to know someone is there that cares!

Consider a "maintenance training" package. Depending on what you plan on doing with your horse on weekends you might want to consider having a trainer or exercise rider take them out for a hack at least three times a week. Horses were not made to stand all week only to come out on weekends and be ridden into the ground. Horses need to keep their tendons strong and their stamina up for most activities, be it a trail ride or a play day. Failure to keep your horse fit opens the door for all kinds of injuries from pulled tendons that can take a year to heal to lifelong issues such as tying up or life threatening issues like colic or founder.

Have realistic expectations. You think you're going to go to the Olympics on a horse that only gets worked on the weekends? Think again. Even if the horse is kept in training, if you want to be a serious competitor, riding only twice a week will not give you the experience or the physical expertise to go that far. And if your horse isn't in full training you can forget keeping that edge that riding your horse daily will give to you both physically and mentally.

Is your horse still green? Don't expect your horse to learn quickly by working with him only once or twice a week. What will happen is the both of you are more likely to experience a good bit of frustration and expecting him

150

to "get it" with inconsistent work is a rather cruel way to treat him. A young horse deserves better and if he is to learn he must have a routine, because being able to rely on you is necessary to build the connection to people that will serve him for the rest of his life.

Be prepared. Even if you know your horse has been turned out and attended to daily, if he hasn't been "worked" all week there are things you should do to keep him and yourself safe. Do a thorough check when you first bring him out to tack him up. While you're grooming him take a close look at every part of his anatomy. How's he holding his head? Are his eyes bright and his attitude/behavior normal? How do his legs look? How do they feel? Any swelling, unusual bumps, scrapes, cuts or nicks? Remember, if you haven't seen him all week you can't rely on everyone at the barn to be paying close attention to the details. If he's a "high" energy horse be sure to turn him out or lunge him before you ride to give him a chance to kick up his heels a bit or tell you how he's feeling. You can also take this opportunity to watch him move and check for any soundness issues. Take precautions using protective gear such as tendon or overreach boots when turning out, in case he goes overboard. Start out slow and give your horse ample warm-up time before any strenuous work. I cringe at the thought of someone shooting out the back gate and blasting off up a hill on their horse. That is a recipe for disaster for any horse, but especially for the horse that doesn't get ridden for days at a time.

Look, it's never easy. We know you want to do the best that you can for your horse. If you can only get out to the barn on the weekends, then taking the right precautions will help you keep your horse sound, healthy and happy for a long time. Be smart, sensible and caring about this. Don't yield to the temptation of following a friend that sets a bad example and is inconsiderate of her mount. Do what you know is right for your horse regardless of peer pressure or your lack of experience. If you're not sure, follow your gut and err on the side of caution. Your horse will thank you and you'll be pleased with your discretion.

BARN ANGELS

What Are Barn Angels?

Let me start by saying almost every barn has at least one, although the larger and more commercial the barn the fewer exist, yet they still appear (or at least their work) from time to time when a horse (or owner) is in need. Sometimes in the dark of night, but most often in the daytime, right out in the open, the Barn Angels go about doing their mighty work.

Sometimes we notice what they do (filling up an empty water bucket, readjusting a fly mask or picking up a blanket that has fallen to the ground), but most of the time, while we're out conquering the world, they're back at the barn scrubbing out water barrels, digging out wet spots and even fly spraying the horses with their own expensive fly spray. I have friends that spend their entire day taking care of other's horses, (people they don't even know) without saying a word for credit. Who are these people? They are simply everyday people like you and me with an extraordinary love for all animals, but gravitate to the horses because circumstances leave most horses (whether they're in a stable or out in a pasture) alone, sometimes for days, without human interaction or having crucial needs met because of it.

Most people, and indeed most owners, underestimate the serious nature of a horse being left alone. Something as simple as a twisted blanket can wreck havoc upon a horse's body, as well as his mind. Leave him wrenched up for days in such a state and you can ruin a horse for life, yet I see it all the time; the blanket strap has come free, the blanket twists lengthening the strap to the ground, the horse steps on it, twists it up more and before you know it the horse is hogtied with something clutching and pulling around its neck like a cougar that has sprung upon him from an overhead branch. At best, this predicament is just until dawn and feeding time, but many horses live in large areas and in backyards going sometimes for days without a single glance from a human. People think as long as their horse has ample food and a water source he'll be fine. THEY WOULD BE WRONG!

In come the Barn Angels to the rescue! They swoop in as soon as they arrive giving the entire barn the once over to check for such problems and then right to work they go; for most have a routine which often starts with water buckets because they recognize its importance. After the water, they travel down a long daily checklist of what needs to be attended to that most likely won't be addressed unless by them. And so it goes without a word to anyone on how hard they've toiled all day. In fact, often their tireless efforts remain a mystery until illness or a move keeps them from the barn and all of a sudden things are in disarray, horse's are colicking and all kinds of mishaps persist.

Are you one of these Angels? If so, you're probably one of the boarders at the stable where your horse is kept or, like me, the trainer at a facility where it's not your job to look after those who are not in training with you but that doesn't matter, only that the horse is cared for properly, so on top of all of your hours spent caring for your client's horses and your personal horses, you look after all the others, as well.

There are owners that resent you for doing anything for their horse, but you don't let that deter you; you understand that it's not about your interaction at all, it's about the guilt that they live under knowing they should do more for their own horse, that they should have been there for him when in need and they were not. So you continue on, determined to be there, because it's only about the horse's needs.

I know in writing this that I am "preaching to the choir" but if in case you are reading this as an absentee owner, I admonish you next time you go out to the stables to see your horse, look around. Who's always the one that's there? Who's always there to answer to how your horse was that day? If it's the same person (or persons) that seem to be most present, chances are you are dealing with a bona fide Barn Angel. I urge you to recognize that person, give them your fullest support and unyielding gratitude, (that is if you care even the slightest bit for your horse) because they are there when you are not. They've spent countless hours caring for YOUR horse! Ask yourself, "where would you be without them?" or more importantly, where would your horse be? (Remember, it's not about YOU anyway.)

So the next time you're at the barn, seek out that person(s). Shake their hand, pat them on the back, hand them a gift, (maybe a nice bottle of wine?) and thank them for being there. Believe me when I tell you they are you and your horse's best friend! And what wouldn't you do for a good friend?

THE HORSE RULES

I'm certain we've talked about some of these things in various chapters throughout this book, but I feel these are so important that it will serve you to have them listed together to reiterate their importance. While some of these things may seem insignificant, and quite possibly you go around each day breaking them, they are called "RULES" for a reason. Break one and you might get away unscathed but keep doing it and eventually you'll be paying a price far greater than you care to. So let's get started and prevent some disasters! Note: These are not listed in order of importance and they all come with certain penalties.

Never teach your horse to open a gate. I learned this many years ago when we thought it was cute to let one of our lesson horses open our arena gate as we rode out of it. Her name was Micha and she was a very large, head strong Appaloosa mare. You may know the type, one that aims to please and figures she knows everything. She took right away to being in charge of letting herself out so she could make her way back to the barn. The problem came when one day I went to open the gate from on her back. Before I could do so she pushed it with so much force that because it was still latched to the railing the entire length of fence line for the arena gave way and fell to the ground. Very embarrassing and a real nuisance but I was grateful there were no kids with me in the ring because their mounts would have certainly taken advantage of their instant freedom.

Never tie to something that could break. I hardly know where to begin with this one but I'll share an example of something that was completely terrifying. I was at a professional facility and noticed a girl tying her horse up to the bars on the door of her box stall. She left to go into her tack room for a bit but before I could follow her to warn her of the danger (she probably wouldn't have listened anyway) the horse pulled back and pulled the barn door right off of its runner. Now she had a crazed Thoroughbred running around the stable with a heavy steel door dangling from its chin as it crashed into everything including the horse itself. This happened many years ago and to be honest I don't recall who had finally caught the horse, I only remember how scared he was and the fear we all felt not knowing how things would end up.

Always open the gate out. Whether you're going in or out of your stall or any enclosure to avoid getting your horse hung up on the gate, open it away from you. We don't always have the choice, but when it's there, take it. This is especially important for children handling ponies. They forget that there's plenty of horse to fit through, and are often not paying enough attention to avoid a mishap.

If there's any way a horse can get hurt they'll find it. This is the harshest reality. If your horse is allowed to be in an area where there are hazards such as broken glass, wire, plastic, wood, nails, ropes, misc equipment just lying around, etc… it's not a matter of whether they'll get hurt, it's just a matter of when. It's hard enough to keep a horse safe in anything other than a padded stall. Just the slightest screw sticking out or wire exposed will pose a safety hazard. I can tell you of countless times when I've found a horse with some abrasion or lump and not a clue as to how it got there.

If your footing is hard for you to run across, it will be hard for your horse as well. Whether your footing is hard and packed or soft and too deep, if it doesn't feel good to you it won't to him. I had a client who decided to take the plunge and buy an amazing horse property in a very desirable area. She wanted only the best for her arena and paid a premium for it to be constructed by someone who had been highly recommended. She asked me to come give my opinion on it, which I did by just running across it myself. I was sad to inform her that the footing was too deep. If she worked a horse in it, it would surely suffer some tendon issues. The next day I received a phone call with her telling me that no sooner had she turned out the first horse, it came up lame and later with the prognosis that the horse had indeed bowed a tendon. Be careful with your footing and take into consideration what it is you plan to do in it. It can make a huge difference when assessing risk factors.

Never feed at the cross ties. Actually, if you want your horse to get antsy, tense and anxious while you're trying to brush and tack him up then feed away. Horses have a good memory and learn quickly. When eating treats in the crossties becomes the norm, your horse becomes very distracted and has a hard time standing still long enough for you to do whatever it is you're there for. Also you must be careful doing this if you board at a stable. Few owners want to contend with their horse becoming anxious because you're treating your horse next to theirs or leaving traces of snacks at his feet. Such a practice is not being a good neighbor.

Always feed at the same time. Horses are creatures of habit and what time of day they eat is a big one. Look, their whole world revolves around food and they get quite excited over the occasion. It's not good to stress your horse out by not being on time with his meals. But there's a bigger reason he needs to be fed at the same time each day. When a horse expects his dinner there are enzymes that are triggered in his system that will help him to digest his food more efficiently. There are even experts that think sticking to a schedule can prevent a bout of colic by alleviating a horse's stress and allowing those enzymes to do their work. Horses like routine, especially when it comes to their meal times.

155

Never feed large pellets, carrots or hard cookies that don't break apart easily. Horse's can very easily get hard objects fed to them lodged in their throat causing a condition known as choke. It is very serious and can actually kill a horse, but at best do major, permanent, damage to the horse's esophagus and your wallet with a very costly vet bill, not to mention the emotional distress to you and your horse! If there is ever a question about whether you should or should not feed your horse carrots, cookies or some other treat, opt not to. And for more reassurance, especially for horses that like to "bolt" their food, older horses or horses with dental issues, soaking their pelleted or cubed feed first until it's soggy is always a much better and safer feeding option.

Never feed someone else's horse without permission. This is a big one! There are many horses that are on strict diets, when the wrong thing can make them dreadfully sick or worse. You never want to feed someone else's horse without their explicit permission each time. (What was ok last week might not be ok today). Always ask to be sure! Just recently our own editor Deborah had a well intending boarder at her stable; feed her newest horse some cookies without her knowledge and without her being there. What resulted was a terrifying ordeal with her horse suffering a very severe case of choke and without prompt vet care he could have lost his life. Needless to say there's a sign posted on his stall now but it would have never been necessary if someone hadn't broken the rules.

Always keep a halter and lead on your stall. Living in Southern California means living in wild fire country. Regardless of where you live, there is always the threat of some sort of emergency, natural or otherwise. Having your horse's halter attached to his stall is imperative because if anyone comes to evacuate they don't have the time to run around and look for the correct halters for each of the horses. I've been involved on various occasions with what goes on when a fire is raging nearby and believe me, time is of the essence. Please note however that care must be taken that the lead attached to the halter never becomes untied and dangles into the stall where it can get tangled around a horse's leg. Attach your halter and lead to your horse's stall, but do so in a way to keep it out of the way of your horse getting into trouble with it.

Never turn out horses together. I'll admit it's fun to let your horse have friends but please understand there are risks and unless you're willing to suffer the consequences with the possibility of vet bills due to play time injury antics, you probably shouldn't go there.

Never tie your horse with its reins. Just because it's done in cowboy movies doesn't mean it's a good idea. There are far too many hazards to having anything outside of your control attached to the bit and NEVER clip your horse into the crossties attached to the bit! I saw someone do this once; the horse set back and tore its mouth to pieces.

Always wear gloves when lunging. Even if you're an expert, have been lunging for years and are extremely careful not to let the line wrap around your hand, there will be times when your horse will catch you off guard, quickly run the other way and voila, you've got a problem! It's not just a matter of protecting your hand from rope burns either; it's about keeping all of your fingers attached to your hand! We all hear the horror stories of someone losing a finger, but I actually know someone that did. She wasn't wearing gloves, the horse took off and the line caught a finger and jerked it off of the girl's hand before she knew what had happened.

Always wear your helmet. Ok, I know I wrote a whole chapter on this one but it must be repeated. We all think an accident will happen to someone else because we're too good of a rider or our horse is too well trained but accidents will happen... eh, that's why they're called "accidents!" Personally, I ride a lot of young and squirrely horses and if I have a moment that I'm not sure will turn out to my benefit the last thing I need to worry about is having a helmet on. ALWAYS wear your helmet!

Keep your vet and farrier's phone number handy and post it where people can easily see them. Do I need to elaborate?

Never trot or canter on pavement. Horses weren't meant to do so. Pounding their feet on pavement can give your horse a nice case of laminitis if he doesn't slip and fall down first. It's just a really dumb thing to do.

Always be aware of your reins in your hands when leading your horse. If you let them get too loose and your horse puts its head down he can easily step on them causing horrible pain to his mouth or worse.

Never leave a blanket on your horse when trailering. It doesn't matter how cold or how open your trailer may be. Horses get anxious when traveling. Add a blanket to the equation and you end up with a sick horse. They sweat up too easily when in the trailer and even a light blanket is a risk.

Never leave a horse tacked up in his stall or turn him out with his saddle on. Oh my gosh, seems crazy I know but I've seen people do it, even with the horse's bridle on with reins hanging down!

Never ride your horse up to a drive thru window. Ask Melissa about this one, lol! Who's Melissa? She's a friend that trained with me when she was a kid. One day she and a friend thought it would be fun to ride their ponies into town and go to lunch. The result was one of the horses spooking, slipping and the friend landing on the pavement. Gees...

Always keep grain/supplement cans secure and in a secure place away from midnight tourists. Basically you don't want to be too casual about your grain/supplemental feed cans. If a horse gets loose and eats too much of the wrong thing he can easily colic or end up with laminitis. Leaving your feed cans unsecured is a very dangerous gamble.

If your horse gets away, never reprimand him when you catch him. No matter how frustrated you may be. This used to happen to my daughter and her pony when she was young. Many years later she saw how illogical her behavior had been when she saw a trainer lose a pony and she couldn't catch it for quite some time. When she did she beat it up pretty good which makes one realize... why would he want to let you catch him if he knows he's going to get a beating?

Always loosen the girth/cinch for a bit before taking off the saddle. It's not just a nice thing to do for your horse and a way to aid a prompt cooling out but it allows the blood to more naturally ease back up to the skin preventing your horse from getting a sore back.

Never leave sweat on your horse. Putting your horse away with sweat left on him doesn't just look bad but is quite bad for his skin. Dried sweat is very irritating for your horse and in time can cause sores, fungus and make life rather miserable for him. If you have time to ride him you have time to clean him up afterwards.

So there's my list. I'm sure there are plenty more, but these few should get your mind started on simply being more mindful. We often go around in our lives just not being aware of things around us. Usually, it doesn't affect us much but when you're around horses, that way of living can be a problem. The bottom line is to think before you do anything and if the thought goes through your head that doing something isn't very smart, listen to it! I've seen some of the worst things happen because people just weren't thinking. Be smart, be safe!

HORSE CARE TIPS

There are so many little things to learn that can make a huge difference in caring for your horse on a daily basis. Most of these aren't life changing, although that may just depend on who you talk to. These are not listed in their order of importance because some things mean more to the individual than something else. You be the judge of what helps you the most. Here we go...

1. Keep your grooming box simple, carrying only those items you use on a regular basis.
2. Use a spritz of water or Static Guard on your brush or rag as you groom to cut static.
3. Purchase a spray bottle from the dollar store and fill it with water. Keep it in your grooming box and you'll always have water handy for spraying down your brushes, dampening a rag or giving your horse a body spritz before grooming to help remove loose dirt from his coat.
4. Keep a rake handy to smooth out dirt in front of a jump to check your striding and direction to it.
5. Feeding your horse Apple Cider Vinegar is known to prevent stones. (Check with your vet before doing so.)
6. Feeding garlic powder to your horse is known to help repel flies. (Check with your vet before doing so.)
7. Use traditional toothpaste to clean and polish silver and bits.
8. To remove that pesky dandruff from manes and tails use a touch of Listerine.
9. To keep stall shavings from sticking to your horse's hooves at shows, spritz hooves with a bit of Show Sheen.
10. After body clipping give your horse a bath of mayonnaise to restore natural oils for a shinny coat.
11. Use black shoe polish to safely darken hooves for shows.
12. Use baby oil to clean, condition and bring back the shine to rubber boots.
13. Orange hand cleaner can turn your yellow Oster boots back to white.
14. Stick your foot into a plastic grocery bag to slip into the tightest boot effortlessly while protecting your foot against blisters (you'd be surprised at how comfortable it makes them).
15. Put rubbing alcohol on a cotton ball and rub on the inside of leather boots and bridles to break in and soften the leather.
16. Mix corn oil with hoof oil to make it last longer.

17. Be sure to re-Velcro boots together when putting them away to prolong their usefulness.
18. Keep and thoroughly rinse out two of your personal shampoo and conditioner bottles (or pick up a couple of empty bottles at your local dollar store). Dilute your horse's full-strength shampoo and condition with water using these bottles. This will not only extend your horse's bathing products, but will make it easier to rinse both out of your horse's coat.
19. Use a patterned hose nozzle on your hose when bathing your horse. Experiment to see which setting your horse likes best for his shower or bath.
20. Use nourishing fish oil for a hoof dressing.
21. Keep lower legs and fetlocks trimmed of extra hair to prevent scratches and bacterial infections.
22. Remove scruff from the front of the back legs by washing weekly with Head and Shoulders shampoo or any dandruff shampoo.
23. Paint the soles of a horse's feet with a 50/50 combo of 7% iodine and turpentine to harden his feet. (CAUTION: prevent touching any skin with mixture and use no more than once per week.)
24. Use a can of compressed air to clean velvet show helmets.
25. Purchase a metal trash can from your local home improvement store, or big box retailer, to use to store grain and supplements. Use a bungee cord to secure the lid to the can.
26. Use ziplock sandwich baggies to ration out your horse's daily supplements for a week or a month. They can be easily marked as to the day of the week and it makes giving your horse his supplements a breeze.
27. Use a kitchen food strainer or a pool net to skim debris out of water tubs between water changes, to keep the tubs fresher longer.
28. Use inexpensive cotton gloves with the little nubbies on them to remove excess dirt and dried mud from your horse before grooming, saving you not only time, but sweat labor while giving your horse a nice massage at the same time.
29. During warmer months, use Avon's Skin So Soft on yourself to keep the flies and biting bugs at bay. Use it under your sunscreen if you're going to be in the sun, so you don't burn. (CAUTION: Don't use it on your horse as a fly repellent as they too can get sunburn, as it's an oil with no sun protection).
30. Use baby or children's sunscreen lotion with an SPF of 30 or higher on sensitive white and pink muzzles/noses to prevent sunburn.
31. Use a long-nose fly mask to protect sensitive white blazes and muzzles from sunburn.

32. Use a fly mask with 'ears' to prevent flies and other biting bugs from entering your horse's ears and wrecking havoc.
33. Dilute your favorite fly spray with water in a spray bottle (one part fly spray to the remainder water) and use it to spray inside your horse's stall, being careful not to spray the inside of his feeder or his water tub) to help eliminate flies.
34. Wipe out your horse's feeder daily to help control flies that like to congregate in their feeders.
35. Mount a battery operated fan in your horse's stall, away from nosy muzzles, to help move the air around his stall and keep flies from landing.
36. Hang penny filled bags of water (out of reach of your horse) in sunny places where flies like to congregate. When the sun hits the bags, the reflection of the pennies in the water confuses the flies and they won't land.
37. Horses love to scratch. Make them a full body scratching post by covering a secure and sturdy pole or post in their stall with outdoor carpeting. It stands up well to the weather and has a nice soft, yet durable texture that is perfect for a good body scratch. To maintain it, just brush it off occasionally with your stiff brush.
38. Use a pretty, decorative metal vase or can in your tack room to store your whips and crops to keep them tidy and all in one place.
39. When trail riding, stay visible! Wear brightly colored, reflective clothing, especially if you're planning on venturing out into multi-use areas with cars, bicyclist, pedestrians and of course, other equestrians. Outdoor clothing stores sell a multitude of inexpensive lightweight "yellow" and/or "orange" vests that can be comfortably and safely worn right over your clothing. By being visible when you ride, you help others to see you and it helps people locate you quicker in the event of an emergency.
40. Donate used tack and supplies that are still in good condition, to your reputable, local non-profit horse rescue organization. Your donated goods will directly help needy horses and you'll save a little on your taxes.

ABOUT THE AUTHOR

Millie Chalk has been a professional trainer for over twenty-five years. She has brought generations of students to come to know the wonder and magic of the horse. Some of her students have gone on to compete internationally while many others hold careers in various aspects of the equine industry as veterinarians, breeders, ranchers and even her own daughter as a very successful Eventing trainer. A testimony to Millie's teachings is that many still keep horses as an integral part of their adult lives. Millie's current professional home, Cherokee Ranch in Shadow Hills, CA is owned and operated by a past student that spent her childhood training by Millie's side.

As impressive as that is, most important to Millie is the role and value she has brought to her students through exposure to an equestrian lifestyle. Having served as the catalyst for her students, from all walks of life, to develop the self esteem and confidence needed to create the lives they hold dear today.

For years, students and friends have suggested Millie write a book on some aspect of horse care and training so others might benefit from her experience. It wasn't until three years ago, when a strange and wonderful chain of events began, that enabled her to find her voice as an author with the book *Horse Cents - A Sensible Guide for the Equestrian Enthusiast* being a natural introduction to what will no doubt be many more books to come.

www.ingramcontent.com/pod-product-compliance
Lightning Source LLC
LaVergne TN
LVHW021454080426

835509LV00018B/2281